Fake Money, Real Danger

Fake Money, Real Danger

PROTECT YOURSELF AND GROW WEALTH WHILE YOU STILL CAN

David Wiedemer

Robert A. Wiedemer

Cindy S. Spitzer

WILEY

Published by John Wiley & Sons, Inc., Hoboken, New Jersey.
Published simultaneously in Canada.

For general information on our other products and services or for technical support, please contact our Customer Care Department within the United States at (800) 762-2974, outside the United States at (317) 572-3993 or fax (317) 572-4002.

Wiley also publishes its books in a variety of electronic formats. Some content that appears in print may not be available in electronic formats. For more information about Wiley products, visit our web site at www.wiley.com.

Library of Congress Cataloging-in-Publication Data

Names: Wiedemer, David (John David), author. | Wiedemer, Robert A., author.
  | Spitzer, Cindy S., author.
Title: Fake money, real danger : protect yourself and grow wealth while you
  still can / David Wiedemer, Robert A. Wiedemer, Cindy S. Spitzer.
Description: Hoboken, New Jersey : Wiley, [2021] | Includes index.
Identifiers: LCCN 2021020643 (print) | LCCN 2021020644 (ebook) | ISBN
  9781119818076 (cloth) | ISBN 9781119818090 (adobe pdf) | ISBN
  9781119818083 (epub)
Subjects: LCSH: Finance, Personal. | Financial crises. | COVID-19 Pandemic,
  2020-
Classification: LCC HG179 .W52645 2021 (print) | LCC HG179 (ebook) | DDC
  332.024—dc23
LC record available at https://lccn.loc.gov/2021020643
LC ebook record available at https://lccn.loc.gov/2021020644

Cover design: Paul McCarthy
Cover image: GETTY IMAGES | Jeffrey Coolidge
SKY10030231_120321

Contents

Preface
Why We Wrote This Book Now

Why now? Why did we wait five years after *Aftershock*, 4th edition (Wiley, 2015) to write a new book?

Well, because this is the perfect time for this new book! And it wasn't before.

Why not?

Honestly, there wasn't much new to write about until now. The economy, although full of vulnerable bubbles, was still going strong. The stock and real estate markets were rising ever higher after the election of President Trump. Most importantly, the Federal Reserve was massively reducing its previous money printing, which had been launched after the 2008 global financial crisis.

When everything is looking good, it's hard to make the case – however accurate – that we are destined for ever higher and higher amounts of money printing to keep the stock market and other bubbles afloat.

Yes, the deficit increased enormously from 2015 to 2019, but nobody cared. It wasn't negatively affecting the markets.

So, it wasn't any easier in 2019 to predict when the Aftershock would begin than it was when *Aftershock* 4th edition came out in 2015.

Every time during those five years that our publisher, John Wiley, and other publishers tried to push us to write a new book, we told them we would – as soon as the Fed was forced to print money again. We knew that, sooner or later, the Fed would be forced to print more money to support the stock market bubble and the rest of our bubble-based economy.

Sure enough, we were right. And, *Oh My God,* did they start rolling the printing press! In March 2020, to save the stock market and the rest of our bubble economy during the Covid-19 pandemic, the US Federal Reserve printed more money in just one week than it printed in an entire year during the Financial Crisis peak.

And the printing presses keep rolling. As of summer 2021, the Fed is printing more than $120 billion per month.

Of course, the Fed could change over the next few years and print less money than it is now, but it will likely still be printing a lot of money in the future for reasons we explain in Chapter 4 (*Hint:* supporting the bubbles).

Hence, we have a much better idea now than any time in the last five years of what forces are likely to finally drive bubble-popping inflation and kick off the coming Aftershock.

We are pleased and proud to present you this new book of insights and advice on what is truly one of the most historic times in world economic and financial history.

Enjoy!

Acknowledgments

The authors thank John Silbersack of The Bent Agency for his relentless support of this book and Kevin Harreld for his work in putting this project together for John Wiley. We thank John Wiedemer, Seline Wiedemer, and Arda Unal for their work on the graphics and data collection. A very heartfelt thanks go to David Pugh, John R. Douglas, and Eric Janszen for their very special roles in making our books a reality.

David Wiedemer

I thank my co-authors, Bob and Cindy, for being indispensable in the writing of this book. Without them, the book would not have been published and, even if written, would have been inaccessible for most audiences. I also thank Dr. Rod Stevenson for his long-term support of the foundational work that is the basis for this book. Dr. Jeff Williamson and Dr. Lee Hansen also provided me with important support in my academic career. And I am especially grateful to my wife, Betsy, and son, Benson, for their ongoing support in what has been an often arduous and trying process.

Robert Wiedemer

I, along with my brother, want to dedicate this book to our mother, who inspired us to think creatively and see the joy in learning and teaching. We also dedicate this to our father, the original author in the family, and to our brother, Jim, for his lifelong support of the ideas behind this book.

I want to thank early supporters Mike Larsen, Steve Schnipper, Ron Everett, Sam Stovall, and Phil Gross. I am most grateful to Weldon Rackley, who helped my father to become an author and who did the same for me.

Of course, my gratitude goes to Dave Wiedemer and Cindy Spitzer for being, quite clearly, the best collaborators you could ever have. It was truly a great team effort. Most of all, I thank my wife and two wonderful children for their support of me and this book.

Cindy Spitzer

Thank you, David and Bob Wiedemer, once again for the honor of collaborating with you on our seventh book. I look forward to many more. For their endless patience and support, my deep appreciation and love go to my husband, Philip Terbush, and our children, Chelsea, Anya, and Zachary. I am also filled with a lifetime of gratitude for two wonderful teachers, Christine Gronkowski (SUNY Purchase College) and two-time Pulitzer Prize winner Jon Franklin (UMCP College of Journalism), who each in their own way helped move me along an amazing path.

CHAPTER 1

Fake Money, Real Danger – Massive Covid Stimulus Boosted the Boom and Will Bring on the Bust

I f a book called *Fake Money, Real Danger* sounds a bit scary, let's make two things clear at the start.

First and foremost, *the potential future dangers described in this book are not happening right now.* The enormous level of government stimulus from massive money printing and borrowing (Fake Money), and the likelihood that Congress will keep borrowing and the Federal Reserve will keep printing, will keep us in high cotton, for now. Even if the stimulus declines, interest rates will stay low and asset prices will likely keep rising.

That means, at least for now, the sky is not falling. Not only is there no reason to panic, investors today still have enormous opportunities – if they move quickly and correctly in the near term.

And that brings us to the second critically important point: *The near term will not last forever.* All this Fake Money, and the asset bubbles it helps create, are not permanent. There is real danger ahead, and only those who see it coming and know what to do about it will be able to hang on to whatever gains they made earlier.

The purpose of this book is not to scare you into inaction, or to scare you into defensive actions that may not actually protect you. Through facts and charts, we want you to see for yourself the full degree and threat of Fake Money. Even better, you can see for yourself when the real danger will begin and what you can do about it.

While the full extent of the future is unknowable, we have developed a way to make substantial gains in the current Fake Money stock market, as well as how to protect yourself from the inevitable failure of the Fake Money economy.

Let's begin.

Just Like the 2008 Financial Crisis, Only Much, Much Worse

Remember the 2008 Financial Crisis? The housing bubble popped, stocks crashed, banks tanked, and the government responded with massive money borrowing and massive money printing – quintupling (five times) the US money supply.

As a result of such massive government borrowing and printing, many businesses and banks were bailed out, the economy eventually recovered, and the sagging stock market resumed its upward rise.

If that sounds a lot like what has been happening during the Covid Crisis, you're not wrong. Only this time the truly massive government stimulus – and the real danger it creates – is even bigger. Much, much bigger.

Congress Borrowed a Massive Amount of Money and Gave It to Everyone

Unlike during the Financial Crisis, when Congress primarily borrowed money to bail out financial institutions and banks, in the Covid Crisis, Congress borrowed unprecedented amounts of money in a very short period of time and gave it to just about everyone.

That's very different from the past, when much of the corporate and financial bailout money was eventually paid back. This time, Congress couldn't care less about getting repaid. It simply borrowed $3 trillion and gave it all away, no strings attached.

To put this giant giveaway into perspective, $3 trillion is about three-quarters the size of the entire government's annual budget. It's also about 15% of our GDP. So, even if our GDP had declined as much as 15% due to the Covid pandemic, there would be relatively little impact because Congress made up for all of it with so much borrowed money.

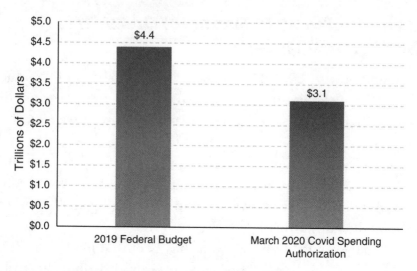

Figure 1.1   Huge Fake Money Giveaway in March 2020

Source: Federal Reserve Bank of St. Louis.

Covid relief spending authorized by Congress in March 2020 was almost as big as the federal government's entire annual budget in 2019.

In fact, in just two months in 2020, Congress authorized borrowing an amount almost equivalent to the entire federal budget for the year (Figure 1.1).

This level of borrowing is totally different from the government's Financial Crisis response and much more powerful in its short-term positive impacts. Unfortunately, it will be much more powerful in its long-term negative impacts, as well.

Of course, few in Congress care about, or even see, any long-term negative impacts. Ask almost anyone in Congress if they expect the massive amount of money to be paid back and they will tell you no – and it doesn't matter if we don't.

And it's not just Congress. Most economists (who should know better) and most investment analysts (who should want to know better) think the same way: we are never going to pay it back, and there's nothing to worry about.

To Support All This Government Borrowing (and the Stock Market), the Fed Printed Massive Amounts of Money

Massive borrowing by Congress was made possible by massive money printing by the Federal Reserve. And if you think the Fed's massive money printing during the Financial Crisis was enormous, take a look at how much *more* massive money printing occurred (so far) during the Covid Crisis (Figure 1.2).

We call all this massive money printing and borrowing Fake Money because it wasn't created in proportion to real economic growth. Instead, it was created in enormous quantities to artificially boost economic activity and, most importantly, to support asset values.

The more Fake Money that we continue to borrow and print, the faker all this Fake Money becomes, creating

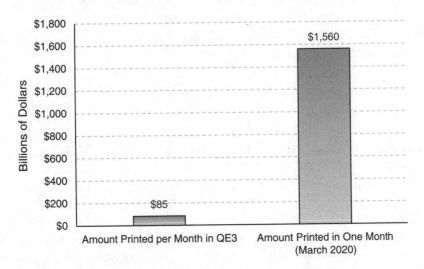

Figure 1.2   Much More Money Printing in the Covid Crisis than the Financial Crisis

Source: Federal Reserve Bank of St. Louis.

In QE3 (the most recent previous round of money printing), the Fed printed about $85 billion of new money per month. In March 2020, money printing shot up to more than $1.5 trillion in just ONE month.

vulnerable asset bubbles and vulnerable bubble wealth. And that's exactly what's been happening during the Covid boom.

How We Know It's Fake Money: A Quick Look at the 1980 Chrysler Loan

Remember the government bailout of Chrysler in 1980? You might not, but it was a big deal then. Chrysler was asking for a $1 billion loan to get it through one of the toughest recessions this country had faced since World War II. Lots of people in Congress were skeptical. Even David Stockman, a young congressman whose congressional district in Michigan had a large Chrysler factory in it. In fact, he was so skeptical that he voted against it.

The debate was months long and tortuous. Many people agreed with Representative Stockman. They didn't want the government to get involved in bailing out private industry. Again, it wasn't a bailout, it was actually a loan. Despite lots of opposition and months of debate, in the end, it passed. And, it was paid back completely – early.

Thirty years later, in 2008, the question of bailing out almost every industry came before Congress. The banking and financial industries were at the top of the list, but the auto industry was there, too. It would take a lot of money – *over $1 trillion*, not $1 billion. Yet, unlike the extremely modest $1 billion Chrysler loan, there was only a month of debate and not much opposition.

Only a little more than 10 years after that, in 2020, Congress approved a *$3 trillion* giveaway with about a month's debate. It wasn't an industry bailout that could potentially be repaid or a loan that must be repaid; it was mostly a massive giveaway. And, it wasn't $1 billion, or $1 trillion. It was $3 trillion, decided quickly with no strings attached, that faced little opposition from Congress or the President.

Why almost no debate over a $3 trillion giveaway but so much debate over a $1 billion loan? Because everyone knows it is absolutely critical to quickly protect the economy and high asset prices from any significant threat. It is a silent recognition of just how fragile those high asset prices really are, and just how dependent the economy really is on those high asset prices. Without this massive influx of Fake Money, there is no solid economic or financial support for such high asset prices. These are bubbles, and they absolutely must have outside artificial government Fake Money support or they will collapse – immediately.

"Now we just have to sit back and wait for the Fed to bail us out."

All This Government Stimulus, Plus Investor Enthusiasm, Created a Massive Stock Market Boom

The Fed's massive money printing during the Covid Crisis helped make the government's massive borrowing possible, kept interest rates low, and pushed the stock market bubble up and up (Figure 1.3).

Some stocks did even better. Tesla, for example, roared up 1800%, moving from $50 per share in mid-October 2019 to almost $900 per share in January 2021 (Figure 1.4).

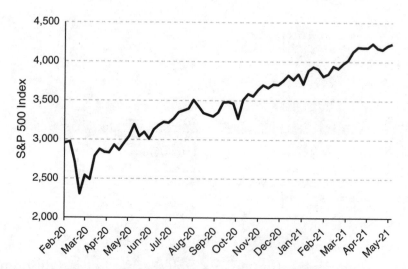

Figure 1.3   Covid Fake Money Was Great for the Stock Market

Source: Standard & Poor's.

The S&P 500 rocketed higher during the Covid Crisis from March 2020 onward.

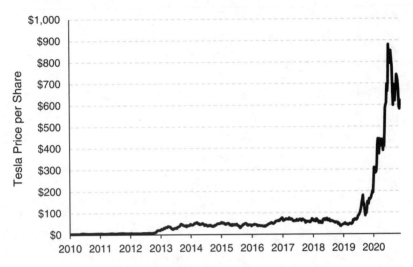

Figure 1.4   Kaboom! Tesla's Stock Price Explodes in the Pandemic

Source: Standard & Poor's.

It's been almost 14 years since the first Tesla car rolled off the assembly line, but almost 95% of its stock value as of June 2021 was created in the 20 months prior, during the Covid pandemic.

All This Stimulus, Plus the Massive Stock Boom and Super Low Interest Rates, Created a Massive Housing Price Boom

In some ways, the Covid Crisis housing price boom has been even bigger than the housing price boom before the 2008–2009 Financial Crisis, with pandemic home prices going sky high in some areas (Figure 1.5).

But, of course, the "experts" will tell you that it's different this time. Unlike the Financial Crisis housing boom, when home prices shot up in a bubble that eventually popped, *this* housing boom is supposedly based on real demand, not just

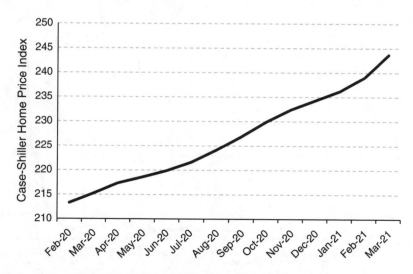

Figure 1.5   Home Prices Go Sky High During the Covid Crisis

Source: Standard & Poor's.

Unlike the Financial Crisis, when housing prices fell 27% from June 2006 to February 2012, housing prices immediately went UP 15% in just 12 months following the Covid Crisis.

bubble frenzy demand that will quickly collapse. Of course, everyone forgets that they assumed the housing demand in 2005–2007 was very real, too – until it collapsed in 2008.

All This Massive Stimulus and Boom Mentality Creates Enormous Opportunities for Investors . . . for Now

This boom ain't over. There's still a lot of money to be made. Chapter 5 describes in detail how to take advantage of the pandemic boom. It makes no sense to miss out on gains now just because we know the Fake Money boom won't last forever.

But it also makes no sense to take advantage of opportunities now and then lose it all later. To optimize your opportunities now, you must also be aware of the real dangers ahead. As you will see later in the book, all this borrowing and printing comes at a very high future price.

To understand the real dangers, it's important to understand that it's not just a Covid Crisis–driven borrowing and printing binge. Unfortunately, our problem is much bigger than anything we did in 2020. In fact, it's been building over many years. The Covid Crisis has just made it worse. A LOT worse.

The Stock Boom Didn't Start with Covid, It's Been Building for a Long, Long Time

While many might prefer not to face it, just a quick glance at the following chart immediately reveals that the US stock market is clearly in an enormous bubble. In the 54 years from 1928 to 1982, the Dow rose a justifiable 300% due to strong long-term economic growth.

However, over the next four decades, the Dow increased an astonishing 3500%, rising from about 1,000 at the end of 1982 to almost 35,000 in mid-2021 (Figure 1.6).

Why? Did company earnings also grow 3,500% in that time? Did the economy grow 3,500%? What about other possible drivers of economic growth and rising stock market values? Did income or population grow 3,500%?

Absolutely not.

Nothing that would normally drive the growth of the stock market grew by 3,500% in 40 years. Instead, the stock market shot up, up, up due to a rocket fuel mix of investor speculation, ultra-low interest rates (created with massive money printing), and massively increasing government and corporate debt.

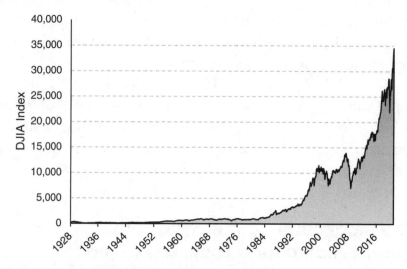

Figure 1.6   The US Stock Market Bubble 1982–2021

Source: Dow Jones.

From 1928 to 1982 the Dow rose about 300%. But from 1982 to mid-2021, the market has risen 3500%! That's far faster than the US economy has grown, or company earnings have risen. In addition to investor animal spirits, much of the increase is due to ultra-low interest rates.

The Housing Boom Didn't Start with Covid – It's Been Building for a Long, Long Time

Driven over the years by low interest rates that kept mortgage loans cheap, and a rising stock market that kept buyers feeling flush, residential and commercial real estate values began to grow much faster than their fundamental drivers of economic and wage growth (Figure 1.7).

As the real estate and stock bubbles both grew bigger over the years, they created much of the fake wealth that we enjoy in our Fake Money economy today.

Even the partial pop of the housing bubble that led to the 2008 global financial crisis did not end the real estate bubble. Low interest rates and rocketing stock prices, especially in 2013 and beyond, helped re-ignite real estate price growth.

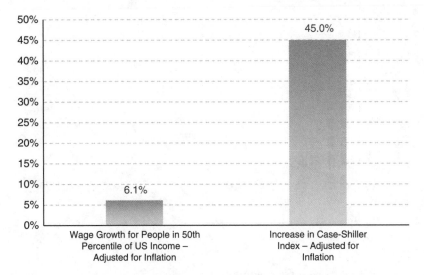

Figure 1.7   Home Price Growth (the Case-Shiller Index) vs. Wage Growth (adjusted for inflation), 1980–2020

Source: Standard & Poor's and the US Bureau of Labor Statistics.

Adjusted for inflation, wage growth for middle-income Americans grew only 6% in 40 years, while home prices rose 45% in the same time period.

Through the years, these co-linked stock and real estate bubbles have been rising together in an upward virtuous spiral of increasing Fake Money.

Massive Government Borrowing Didn't Start with Covid – It's Been Building for a Long, Long Time

When our first book came out in 2006, our federal debt of $8.5 trillion was huge and unsustainable relative to our economic growth, and the odds of paying it back were near zero. All the government could do was refinance this debt again and again by borrowing more and more, growing the federal debt bubble ever larger.

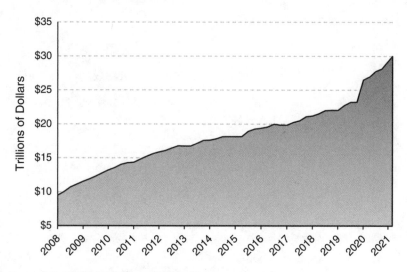

Figure 1.8   US Federal Debt, 2008–2021

Source: Federal Reserve Bank of St. Louis.

The monster federal debt bubble has climbed steeply since the 2008 Financial Crisis from about $10 trillion in 2008 to over $30 trillion in 2021.

However, back in 2006, it seemed unthinkable that in just 15 years the total federal government debt would more than triple to *$30 trillion* by 2021 (Figure 1.8). This is now an impossibly gigantic bubble from which there is no return. All we can do at this point is borrow even more so we can keep refinancing the debt and keep paying for massive government spending.

And now, in the throes of the Covid pandemic, this expanding monster of a bubble has moved into hyperdrive. Shockingly, we added more new federal debt just in June 2020 than the debt increased in *all* of 2019 (Figure 1.9).

Huge federal debt can go on for a long time without consequences. But once massive money printing eventually causes rising inflation (see Chapter 3), interest rates will also rise significantly causing an asset bubble collapse.

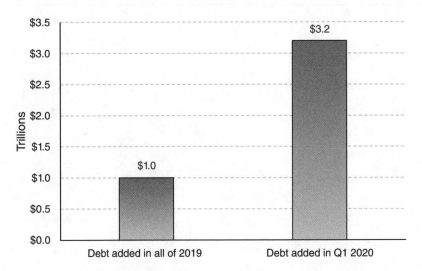

Figure 1.9   Federal Debt Added in 2019 vs. Debt Added in Q1 2020

Source: Federal Reserve Bank of St. Louis.

New federal debt added in just the first quarter of 2020 dwarfs the amount of new federal debt added in all of 2019.

That is not happening now or soon, but to pretend it can't or won't happen ever is premeditated bubble blindness.

Massive Money Printing Didn't Start with Covid – It's Been Building for a Long, Long Time

Driving up, supporting, and maintaining all the other enormous bubbles, especially the stock market and federal debt, is the massive and ever-growing money-printing bubble.

Prior to the 2008 financial crisis, the US money supply weighed in at $800 billion. Today, after several rounds of post-2008 massive money printing and even more massive rounds of money printing in 2020, the Federal Reserve has mega-printed *more than $7 trillion* – increasing the money supply almost *ten times* in just 12 years (Figure 1.10).

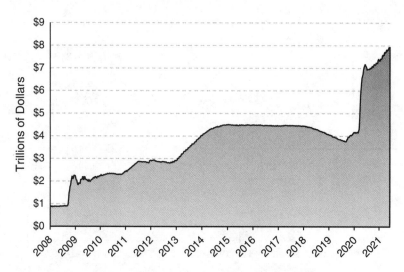

Figure 1.10   The Massive Money Printing Bubble, 2008–2021

Source: Federal Reserve Bank of St. Louis.

The Federal Reserve has expanded the money supply by almost 900% to boost the stock market and economy after the 2008 Financial Crisis.

The US economy would have lost all its bubbles long ago, had there not been a gigantic increase in newly printed dollars. The Fed has been free to print new money in order to manipulate, grow, and maintain our vulnerable multibubble economy. In doing so, the Fed has helped kick the inevitable bubble-popping can down the road. Massive money printing directly helps pump up the bubbles. Without it, the stock market and other bubbles would have already popped.

Corporations Are Also Driving the Stock Market Boom with Massive Stock Buybacks, Especially During the Pandemic

It's not just the government that is pushing up the stock market bubble. Corporations are driving up the stock market as well. Since 2008, when the Federal Reserve greatly lowered

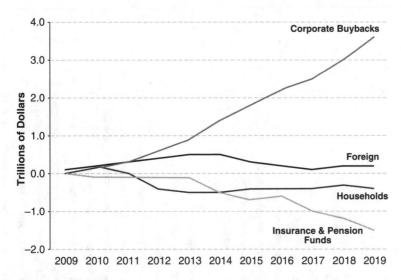

Figure 1.11   Buy, Buy, Buy: Corporations the Only Net Buyer of Stocks, 2008–2019

Source: Goldman Sachs.

Since the 2008 Financial Crisis, corporations have been the ONLY net buyer of stocks. Without those corporate buybacks, the market would have seen massive net-selling and big downward pressure.

interest rates, corporations have borrowed oodles of money at ultra-low interest rates to *buy back their own stock*. The large and growing corporate debt bubble created the corporate stock buyback bubble that helped push the stock market bubble up even faster and higher.

This huge stock buyback bubble has been critically important to the stock market. In fact, from 2008 to 2019, corporations have been the *ONLY* net buyer of stocks (Figure 1.11).

In other words, without corporate stock buybacks, the huge stock market bubble might very well have popped by now.

The corporate buyback bubble looks set to continue inflating at a rapid pace. In 2021, with continued ultra-low interest rates, corporate buybacks are expected to hit their highest level in 20 years (Figure 1.12). All good for stocks. Party on!

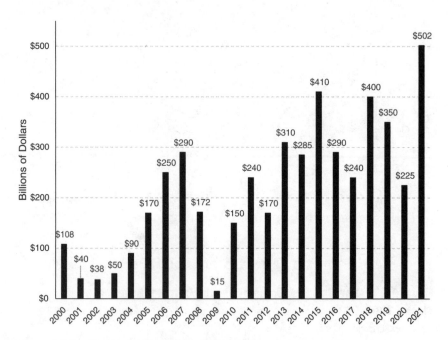

Figure 1.12   Corporate Buybacks 2000–2021

Source: Goldman Sachs.

Corporate buybacks in 2021 are expected to hit the highest level in 20 years.

But There's a Catch – All This Pandemic Stimulus, Piled on Top of All the Earlier Massive Borrowing and Printing, Is Creating Real Danger: Fake Money

Not sure we are creating lots of Fake Money? Maybe you're thinking that we can keep borrowing money and NEVER pay it off, or we can keep printing money and NEVER get inflation. Or maybe you're thinking it's only a *little problem.* Or maybe our Fake Money is just a *little bit fake.*

Maybe you think our exceptionally wealthy economy is big enough and strong enough to handle a lot of artificial stimulus and we don't have to worry about borrowing and printing so much money? Most people seem to be assuming (or at least hoping) that is true.

But what if it isn't true? What if you were able to quickly and easily see what most people – even most economists – refuse to see? Our economic growth is *fake,* and our wealth, which is based on the assumption that artificial government stimulus creates real value, is also quite fake, like the money being printed to support it.

Come now to Chapter 2, and in just a few more pages you will get a better picture of just how fake that economic growth, and asset values, really are.

Fake Money, Fake Wealth?

Chapter 1 asserted that the government's response to the Covid pandemic with massive money borrowing and massive money printing has created an enormous boom, pushing up stocks and real estate.

We call all this borrowing and printing "Fake Money" because it was (and continues to be) produced rapidly and in massive amounts for the explicit purpose of revving the economy and artificially supporting the markets. Plenty of Fake Money was also created during the Financial Crisis, but nothing like the truly mega amounts of Fake Money created during Covid.

The near-term benefits of Fake Money are palpable: surging economic growth, new stock market highs, and booming home prices. But the longer-term risks of so much Fake Money are highly dangerous because Fake Money creates *fake wealth.*

The idea that our wealth is as fake as the Fake Money that is creating it, is a bit hard for most people to swallow. Many people would agree that we cannot borrow massive amounts of money and NEVER pay it back. And many would agree that we cannot print massive amounts of money and NEVER get inflation. But maybe, just maybe, we can hope against hope that our Fake Money is creating real wealth – the kind of wealth that will last long term.

Unfortunately, as you are about to see, the damning evidence says otherwise.

Stunning Proof That Our Wealth Is Fake

Sometimes the most glaring evidence is hiding in plain sight while no one says a word.

Here's something you won't hear from economists or investment experts: Almost all economic growth in the United States since the 2008 Financial Crisis has been entirely the result of massive government borrowing. *Almost all of it.*

You might have suspected that to be true in 2020, given the massive government pandemic spending, but it's hard to believe that is true for all the years since the 2008 Financial Crisis.

But the data shows it very clearly (Figure 2.1). Let's take a look at GDP growth in 2020. It was worse than you think. Sure, you might have suspected the economy didn't grow in 2020, which is true. But did you know that without the massive government borrowing our economy would have declined by almost 20%.

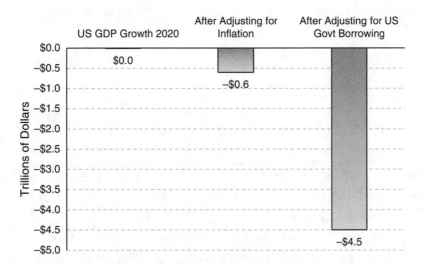

Figure 2.1   Economic Growth (GDP) in 2020 Adjusted for Government Borrowing and Inflation

Source: Federal Reserve Bank of St. Louis.

In 2020, instead of showing no growth, our economy would have actually declined almost 20% without massive government borrowing.

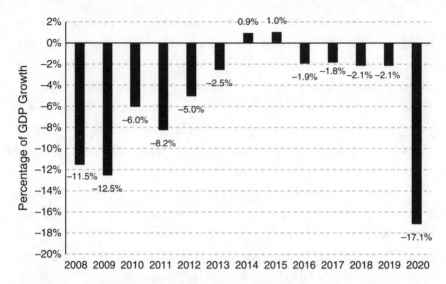

Figure 2.2   Economic Growth (GDP) 2008–2020, Adjusted for Government Borrowing and Inflation

Source: Federal Reserve Bank of St. Louis.

It wasn't just 2020 when ALL of our economic growth came from government borrowing. In fact, that's been true for almost every year since the Financial Crisis.

Even with an enormous rebound in economic growth in 2021, which we expect, it is very unlikely we will have any growth without massive government borrowing.

And that pattern of no growth (when adjusted for government borrowing) is not likely to change in 2022, 2023, or 2024. Why? As we said earlier, for the last 13 years we would have had no growth at all without government borrowing. Take a look at Figure 2.2.

This means that "real" economic growth – after it is adjusted for government borrowing and inflation – is practically nonexistent. GDP growth in the United States is an illusion, created by a massive and growing federal debt bubble. Take away the huge numbers of dollars flowing in from government borrowing each year and the US economy has been going nowhere for more than a decade.

Of course, no one ever talks about economic growth in this way. Google it and you will see for yourself that no one compares GDP growth to government borrowing.

Why not?

Because that would instantly reveal what just about everyone wants to avoid facing: *our economic growth is fake.* It all comes from Fake Money (money borrowing). And if our economic growth is fake, that means our wealth that is based on fake economic growth is also fake.

It's ALL Fake Money.

We Know There's Real Danger: A Quick Look at the End of World War II

When World War II ended, the citizens of the US were very happy. It wasn't easy, and it wasn't fun. But we were right, and we won.

But how did we treat the men and women who served our country so well? We fired them. Tens of millions were tossed. Millions in the military and millions more in the industries that supported them.

Who could have been more deserving of a helping hand from our government than these people who worked so hard and risked so much for our country? But did they get massive unemployment benefits larger than their previous wages to tide them over until they found a job? Did the industries who had worked so hard to win the war get bailouts? No.

In fact, relative to people in the Covid economy of 2020 and 2021 they got almost nothing.

Why?

It was simply that we didn't want to borrow the massive amount of money necessary to pay all of these well-deserving people lots of money after the war. Individuals and businesses were on their own to find a way to make a living while the economy moved from a wartime to a peacetime economy.

(Continued)

Again, not because the government didn't want to help these very deserving people. It's just that the government (and our citizens) viewed money from the government as *real money*. To them, it wasn't Fake Money. If the government spent money, it had to get it the old fashioned way – from taxes. If it borrowed money, it needed to pay it back. The government and its citizens knew intuitively that treating money from the government as Fake Money created real danger.

Today, the government hands out money like water bottles. They think it's free. And so do a lot of our citizens. That's largely because, on some level, they know its fake. Give out more money and the government will simply print more of it, right?

What they don't know, or they blatantly ignore, is that Fake Money *ultimately is not free*. It's very, very costly in terrible ways we are guaranteed to eventually see.

It's amazing how much this country has changed since World War II.

More Stunning Proof That Our Wealth Is Fake: We Have 10 Times More Debt Than Tax Revenue

Economists and other "experts" like to talk about our debt as a percentage of GDP. By talking about government debt only as it compares to the entire country's economic output, people can avoid facing the fact that our total debt is tremendously large compared to the government's ability to pay it back.

What exactly is the government's ability to pay it back?

Well, if we were talking about individual or business debt, the ability to pay off debt would surely be a function of that individual or business's *income*. For example, if Joe Smith owes $50,000 and his annual income is $500,000, we would say his ability to pay back his debt is much higher than if he makes only $5,000 a year. At only $5000 in income, Joe is unlikely to ever pay off his $50,000 debt. Certainly, no bank or lender would be willing to lend him more.

The federal government is no different from an individual or a company: the government's income matters. What exactly is the government's income? *Tax revenue!*

So, let's put aside the old debt-to-GDP comparison and get real about our Fake Money. The federal government's total debt is now more than 10 TIMES its income (aka, tax revenue) (Figure 2.3).

Of course, no one talks about debt in this way. Instead of comparing debt to income (tax revenue), everyone loves to keep talking about debt in terms of GDP. And we can certainly understand why!

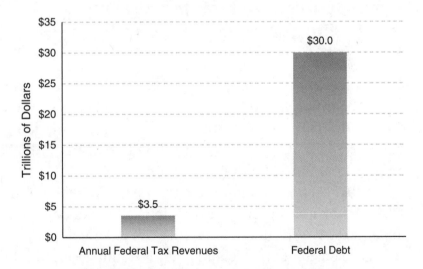

Figure 2.3 Our Government's Debt to Revenue Ratio is almost 10 to 1

Source: Federal Reserve Bank of St. Louis.

The federal government's only source of money (other than Fake Money from money-printing and borrowing) is tax revenue, which is about $3.5 trillion. Our debt is almost $30 trillion. To think we could make an attempt to pay back even part of that debt is laughable.

Imagine if we compared a company's debt to GDP. Everybody would think that's crazy. Let's assume that company is Amazon – do any analysts look at its debt compared to GDP. Of course not! Our GDP doesn't pay Amazon's debt, its revenues do.

And the same is true for the US. We all know that. Unlike Amazon, there's not a hope in hell we can even think about paying back *any* of our federal debt. We won't even try. In fact, we will be forced to borrow fabulously more money.

That's why economists and Wall Street desperately avoid talking about our debt in terms of income (tax revenues). It's all part of our deep reluctance to avoid facing facts we'd rather not face.

We aren't making these numbers up. Anyone can easily find them online. The trouble is, *no one wants to look!*

A Great Solution for Maintaining Our Fake Wealth: Just Print More and More Fake Money!

OK, if the idea that we can ever repay our debt is fake, and if all our GDP growth is fake (because it's all based on borrowed and therefore Fake Money), what in the world are we going to do to keep our asset values (stocks, bonds, real estate) high and protect our Fake-Money-based wealth?

Easy! Just keep printing more and more massive amounts of Fake Money to keep interest rates low so we can pay interest on and rollover (refinance) our massive federal debt!

It's a dream come true. There really is nothing we can't do or any economic problem we can't solve with more and more printed money!

World War II Deficits vs. Today

A number of people respond to today's massive deficits by saying they aren't that much of a problem. We ran big deficits in World War II, and they didn't destroy the economy.

Well, let's take a look at those deficits. They did grow fast. The deficit in 1940 was $3 billion. That doubled to $6 billion in 1941. Then tripled to $23 billion in 1942 and almost tripled again to $65 billion in 1943. It peaked in 1944 at $65 billion. But then decreased in 1945 to $58 billion as the war ended. There was another huge decrease to $10 billion in 1946 and a complete elimination of the deficit by 1947, when we actually ran a surplus of $11 billion!!

How did we do that? We cut spending. A lot. We fired almost everyone working for the military and to support the military. It was that simple.

We don't do that today. We have massive peacetime deficits that go down at times, but, overall, have climbed to higher and higher levels since the 2001 recession.

Even pre-Covid in 2019, we ran a $1 trillion deficit. We run massive deficits every year. It's not at all like World War II. In 1980, our deficit was $45 billion. This year it will be over $2 trillion. This is not a one-time, short-term deficit. It is a long-term economy supporting/asset price supporting deficit that we can't stop without collapsing both those high asset prices and the economy along with it.

The money may be fake, but does that really matter? As long as we can keep printing and borrowing, we can solve all our economic problems, continue to push stock and real estate values beyond the moon, and keep our fake wealth safe and growing larger forever!

There's only one catch . . .

Maintaining Our Fake Wealth by Printing More and More Fake Money Works Great – As Long as We Can Keep Printing Without Creating Inflation

Inflation is the Achilles' heel of massive Fake Money printing and borrowing. If we can avoid significant inflation forever, we can keep printing and borrowing forever. If we cannot avoid significant inflation forever, massive printing and borrowing will eventually be forced to end, and the gig will be up.

That's because high long-lasting inflation will eventually force interest rates up, and high interest rates will kill asset values. Without low interest rates, our Fake Money wealth bubble will be no more. That leaves us with some questions:

- *Will we ever get high, long-lasting inflation, and if so, when?* You can see for yourself in Chapter 3.
- *How much money printing and inflation will it take to pop the Fake Money bubble?* You can play with the numbers and see for yourself on our website www.fakemoneyreal-danger.com (under the tab When Will It Pop?). There you will find an interactive model that allows you to see what happens to your wealth as printed money creates inflation.
- *How can we protect and grow real wealth before it's too late?* You can find lots of details about that in Chapters 4–7.
- *How bad will it get?* That depends on how long it takes for the Fake Money bubble to pop. The more we try to save the Fake Money bubble with more and more Fake Money, the bigger the bubble gets. The bigger the bubble gets, the more we are setting ourselves up for a bigger fall and a much longer time in the economic pits – think decades, not years.

When the Fake Money bubble pops, stocks, bonds, real estate, and privately owned business valuations will collapse. This will cause Americans at every economic level who are not properly protected to see their wealth and standard of living substantially decline.

This is not a theoretical problem. This is a very real problem that every investor – including you – must solve.

Keep reading, and we will show you how.

Fake Money . . . Real Support

There is real danger ahead, and we all need to prepare for what will likely be a devastating blow to investments, livelihoods, and wealth.

For the latest updates as we approach the inevitable Financial Cliff and Aftershock ahead, please visit www .fakemoneyrealdanger.com or www.aftershockpublishing .com.

There you can also sign up to receive any of our email alert services – *all 100% free.*

Or contact us at 703-787-0139 or info@aftershock publishing.com.

For private consulting for individuals, businesses, and groups, please contact *Fake Money, Real Danger* and *Aftershock* coauthor Cindy Spitzer at 443-980-7367 or information@ arksma.com. Your first call is free.

For hands-on investment management based on the macroeconomic views and investment strategies described in our books, please contact Ark Financial Management at 703-774-3520, 888-238-8370 or information@arksma.com.

3

Will We Ever Get High, Long-Lasting Inflation? If So, When?

The government's massive borrowing and money printing (aka, Fake Money) during the Covid Crisis has pushed asset prices up even higher – including stocks and real estate – making investors and homeowners very happy. Naturally, everyone wants their investments and homes to be worth more and more over time, or at least maintain their value.

Unfortunately, as we saw in the last chapter, some ugly truths have been hiding in plain sight, even though no one wants to look. The fact is that nearly all our economic growth since 2008 completely disappears when we account for new government debt (Fake Money) and inflation each year.

If all our economic growth since 2008 had been built on Fake Money, then any wealth built on this fake economic growth is, sadly, also fake.

That last sentence is shocking and very tough to accept. One way we keep from having to fully digest such a terrible possibility is to hope against hope that our current fake wealth will last forever. And with endless government support in the form of continued massive money printing and borrowing, *it will* . . . right up to the point when it can no longer.

When will that happen?

Welcome to Chapter 3.

When Will Our Fake Money Wealth Bubble Pop?

It's a simple question with a simple answer: Our Fake Money bubble will pop when massive money printing finally creates significant, long-lasting *inflation*.

But determining the timing of that is not so simple. Back in the old days (before 2008), excess money printing generally caused inflation in roughly 18 to 24 months, according to dozens of Federal Reserve and non-Fed economic studies in multiple countries over many decades.

That was then. Now we are in a whole new and quite different era in which the old rules don't seem to apply.

In this new era, many people here and around the world think that the United States can massively print money and *never* get significant inflation. And, for more than 10 years, they have been absolutely right. There has been no significant inflation at all.

This has been wonderful, because . . . .

Low Inflation Is Key to Low Interest Rates, and Low Interest Rates Are Absolutely Critical to Maintaining Our Fake Money Wealth Bubble

Maintaining low inflation, despite massive money printing, is critically important for bubble protection because low inflation *keeps interest rates low.*

Low interest rates are great for pushing up the markets (stocks, bonds, real estate). And low interest rates are absolutely essential for maintaining the government's ability to keep borrowing massive amounts of money.

Remember, without massive borrowing we'd have no economic growth at all. Without massive borrowing, government spending would decrease dramatically. And without massive borrowing, we cannot make our interest payments on our outstanding debt. Make no mistake: it's all outstanding debt. We never pay a penny on principal. We just roll over the debt and borrow more – and more. We even borrow to pay the interest. So, we absolutely *must* keep borrowing.

The federal government started significant borrowing as early as the 1980s, but nothing like what we have been borrowing starting with the 2008 Financial Crisis. Normally, such a huge demand for borrowed money would push interest rates up and hurt the economy.

But just the opposite happened. Interest rates didn't rise, they actually fell after the Financial Crisis and dropped even further during the Covid Crisis, despite tremendous government borrowing that has increased the total federal debt to a staggering $30 trillion. Yet interest rates are now down to almost zero.

What gives?

The answer is *massive money printing coupled with LOW INFLATION*. Massive money printing makes money highly available and therefore cheap to borrow. As long as massive money printing doesn't cause significant inflation (or doesn't cause significant inflation for too long), all is well. Maintaining our Fake Money wealth all comes down to *keeping inflation low*.

Keeping Inflation Low Is Key to Continued Massive Borrowing and Printing to Sustain Fake Money Wealth

In the fight to make Fake Money wealth last forever, high inflation is bad and low inflation is good.

High inflation is bad. It eventually drives up interest rates that put downward pressure on stocks, bonds, and real estate, and greatly limits more government borrowing to sustain the Fake Money wealth bubble.

Low inflation is good. It allows the government to continue massive borrowing and printing to sustain and grow

the Fake Money wealth bubble. The benefits of low inflation are many:

- *In the absence of inflation,* the Federal Reserve can print
  massive amounts of new money with no immediate negative consequences. No one really believes in entirely
  unlimited money printing, but the Fed, Congress, and
  investors very strongly support "just the right amount"
  of money printing (like Goldilocks, not too much, not
  too little) to support the financial markets.
- *In the absence of inflation,* massive money printing provides the funds the Fed needs to buy government bonds
  to support the massive government spending without
  the need to attract investors with higher interest rates.
- *In the absence of inflation,* low interest rates made it easy
  for the government to borrow $3 trillion in 2020 and
  2021, and likely another $2–3 trillion next year if it
  wants. In the absence of inflation, massive money printing and low interest rates means the government can
  borrow as much as it wants for as long as they want – as
  long as there is no inflation.
- *In the absence of inflation,* which would put a halt to massive money printing and drive up interest rates, the Fed
  is theoretically free to buy government and other bonds
  indefinitely. There really is no statutory or legal limit on
  how much Fake Money the Fed can print or how many
  government and other bonds the Fed can buy.

There is only one very firm limit on all this money printing
and money borrowing: *inflation!* Significant, long-lasting inflation would absolutely and completely ruin the whole thing.

How "Significant" Would Inflation Have to Get for Fake Money Printing and Borrowing to Hit a Wall?

If inflation were to reach 10%, or even just 5%, investors will become increasingly reluctant to buy government or any other long-term bonds. Why? Because, currently, investors are buying long-term bonds under the assumption that we will see no significant inflation for the next 10–20 years. If that assumption proves wrong, the value of those bond values will fall, and the bond market could easily collapse.

At first, bond investors will likely ignore early moderate inflation. But rising inflation, if it rises enough, would eventually push up interest rates, which drive down bond prices and seriously hurt the bond market.

Surging inflation and rising interest rates would also hurt the stock market. And, of course, rising interest rates would be a big negative for real estate values and the rest of the economy. You may find it worth your time to take a look at *Aftershock* (4th edition) for more details on how high inflation could devastate the economy and nearly all your investments.

Bottom line: no one wants inflation. It would eventually force an end to massive borrowing and money printing.

No one wants that!

The Fate of the US Economy Now Depends on an All-In Bet That We Can Avoid Significant, Long-lasting Inflation Forever

At this point, given the massive amount of government stimulus (money printing and borrowing) both past and present, the future of our Fake Money economy depends on an all-in bet that we will *never get high inflation*.

Our all-in bet has only two possible long-term outcomes:

1. *We get no significant, long-lasting inflation.* Therefore, we can continue to support our Fake Money wealth with more massive money borrowing and printing; or
2. *We get significant, long-lasting inflation; interest rates eventually climb.* Then massive money printing and borrowing is forced to end, and our Fake Money wealth bubble pops.

We have already doubled down on this all-in bet, again and again (especially recently) with more and more massive borrowing and printing, so there's no going back now. Our all-in bet is on!

Given the lack of significant inflation over the last 10 years, many people believe that we've already won this bet. After all, our money supply is up over 1000% since 2008, and the federal debt is now more than $30 trillion, yet inflation is still relatively low.

Recently, some discussion of future inflation has stirred. But very few people among the mainstream media, academic economists, or investment analysts are talking about the potential threat of significant long-lasting inflation. Just about everyone is assuming we will *never* get significant long-lasting inflation.

This lack of concern has some big advantages: Without fear of inflation, there is no need to worry about rapidly rising government deficits in the future.

Avoiding significant inflation forever means the usual negative economic consequences of massive money printing and borrowing simply no longer apply.

Instead, we can print all the money we want, borrow all the money we want, and spend all the money we want!

Sounds Like a Lovely Dream, Doesn't It?

Believe it or not, some respected economists fully believe that this dream is, in fact, real. And there's even a new economic theory to explain it, called *Modern Monetary Theory (MMT)*. An outspoken proponent of MMT, Stephanie Kelton, from Stony Brook University, wrote a *New York Times* article (June 9, 2020) titled "Learn to Love Trillion-Dollar Deficits." She also authored a book promoting massive government borrowing, called *The Deficit Myth*. (A link to her article can be found at https://www.nytimes.com/2020/06/09/opinion/us-deficit-coronavirus.html.)

It provides a good short overview of Modern Monetary Theory. MMT formalizes what we have just described; that the government can borrow and spend as much as it wants because the Fed can print unlimited money to buy an unlimited number of the bonds the government issues to pay for its spending.

Unlike past economic thinking, MMT says the government is now in no way limited in its spending by the amount it can collect in taxes. In fact, based on this theory, one might ask why the government needs to collect taxes at all when it can simply borrow a nearly unlimited amount of money at low cost that it never has to repay.

MMT says that the only limit to government borrowing is high inflation. Well, we completely agree with that – inflation is the only true limit to government stimulus of the economy.

But here's the big difference. MMT says that we will only get inflation when the economy heats up and the demand for goods and services pushes up prices. Interestingly, MMT makes no mention of the real possibility of *stagflation* (inflation plus recession), like what we had in the 1970s and early 1980s. MMT thinks inflation is only the result of rising demand for goods and services, heating up the economy.

That's what a lot of people think! So even though MMT has only limited support among academic economists, and very limited recognition by the public, almost everyone already agrees with it!

Without much discussion, there is an unspoken, almost universal agreement in the basic tenets of MMT among many investors, government officials and economists: We don't have to worry too much about massive government stimulus (in fact, their big worry is that the government will print, borrow, and spend too little), AND inflation will only be a problem if the economy overheats and there is much higher demand for goods and services.

This all sounds very, very good, *but it's not at all true* – not even if everyone really, really hopes it's true. No one wants to see that the future now depends on an all-in bet that is *guaranteed to fail.* It is a lot more comfortable to believe that somehow it will all work out fine later, even if believing that requires maintaining a giant blind spot regarding what inflation is and what actually causes it.

So, let's take a moment now to see what inflation is, and what it is not.

This may surprise you.

"You'll see, this is going to cause <u>real</u> trouble."

What Is Inflation? It's Not What You May Think

It's a common belief that inflation comes from high demand for goods and services, which pushes up prices. However, that is totally untrue. High demand does not push up inflation; instead, it pushes up the *real* price of goods and services. As demand rises, prices will rise which encourages more supply. As supply increases, the price will fall. It's simple supply-and-demand economics.

This is a *price increase* due to growing demand or declining supply or both. It is temporary, lasting only as long as supply and demand are out of balance.

Increasing demand could also force a long-term real price increase by forcing producers to move to higher-cost production to meet demand. Such as moving from cheap oil in Texas to more expensive offshore oil in the Gulf of Mexico or the North Sea.

None of that is inflation!

Real inflation is tricky to understand, but it's like pornography – you know it when you see it, even if a bit hard to define. So, to understand inflation better, let's start with what inflation is NOT.

What Inflation Is NOT

1. *Inflation is not simply an increase in price.* A simple increase in price could be due to a decrease in supply or an increase in demand, and not necessarily due to inflation. This is the kind of price increase you would get in a rapidly growing economy. Yet, we've had a decently growing economy since 2009, and we've had nearly no inflation. And when we had a very slow-growing economy in the late 1970s and early 1980s, we had very high inflation. In fact, rising inflation is actually more associated with a low-growth economy (stagflation). Therefore, inflation is NOT simply an increase in prices.

2. *Inflation is not an increase in prices unmatched by an increase in wages.* You can't have inflation without having wage inflation. If prices are increasing and wages are not, that's not inflation. Wage increases may not keep up with inflation, but they will definitely rise in an inflationary environment.

3. *Inflation is not an increase in wages due to an increase in productivity.* Wages in China increased dramatically between 1990 and 2010. That wasn't inflation. That was due to

rapid increases in productivity. People in China were being paid more because they were more productive per hour of a labor. People in Germany or Japan aren't paid more than people in Mexico or China because they have had higher inflation; they are paid more because they have higher productivity. In fact, higher productivity is the only source of real wage growth.

4. *Inflation is not an increase in asset prices.* Everybody knows that if Apple's stock doubles in value over three years, that's not inflation. That's a very good investment! Same for real estate.

5. *Inflation is not a price increase due to higher production costs.* Clearly this has nothing to do with inflation. For example, the cost of college education has gone up enormously in the last 30 years. Much of that increase is a real price increase, not inflation. Colleges have much higher payroll costs (primarily for more administrative jobs) than they used to, while educating essentially the same number of students. Hence, the cost of educating each student has increased dramatically. That's a real price increase, not inflation.

What Inflation IS

1. *Inflation is an increase in BOTH wages and goods/services prices caused by the government printing more money.* Hence, if the money supply is increasing much faster than the economy, expect inflation to occur.

2. *Inflation almost always occurs in a low-growth economy.* Why? Because that's when governments see both reduced income from taxes and increased outflows due to social-support demands. Hence, not wanting to increase taxes during a bad economy, the government offsets the loss

of tax revenues by printing more money. Money printing (beyond what is needed to keep up with real economic growth) causes inflation.

3. *Inflation is created when countries have tax systems with a
high degree of unreported income or outright fraud.* To offset
the lack of tax revenues, the government continuously
prints much more money than their economic growth
warrants. Again, money printing causes inflation.

Among more developed economies, this is most easily
seen in countries like Turkey, Argentina, and Italy. However, Turkey and Italy have made big strides forward in
reducing this problem. In Italy, in 1980, it took 1 million
lire to buy a bottle of Coke. In Turkey, in 2005, it took
1 million Turkish lire to buy a bottle of Coke. In Turkey
today, it only costs 10 lire to buy a Coke. They still have
double-digit inflation, but it's nothing like it was before.

4. *Inflation is almost always stagflation.* For the above reasons, inflation is almost always stagflation, where the
economy is declining and inflation is rising rapidly.

Most People Think Significant Long-Term Inflation Won't Happen – Unfortunately, They're Wrong

Lack of significant inflation in the last 10 years, despite the
Fed printing enormous amounts of new money, strongly sup-
ports the idea that massive money printing no longer causes
inflation. Not now and not ever again.

Two ways inflation is made less noticeable in the short term
are banks holding excess reserves (reserves that are above
what the Federal Reserve requires them to hold) and statisti-
cal manipulation (by changing the way inflation is calculated).

So, the mild inflation that has already occurred has largely been hidden.

Because investors, government officials, and many economists saw that quintupling (five times) the money supply after the 2008 Financial Crisis did not create inflation, many are now assuming that, for some unknown reason, printing money no longer creates inflation. Certainly, for the last 10 years, that's been absolutely true in the US and other major economic powers.

But the assumption that *delayed* inflation means *no* inflation ever, is wrong. *Way wrong.*

If Money Printing Does Not Create Inflation, Then . . . .

- Why do countries like Argentina and Turkey have inflation now?
- Why did major countries like the US, France, and England have high inflation only a few decades ago? What has changed so that money printing no longer creates inflation in the US or Europe?
- Why don't we print all the money we want and pay off all student loans?
- Why don't we pay off all mortgages?
- Why don't we eliminate all taxes? Just print all the money we need.
- Why don't we give everyone $10,000 (or $100,000) immediately? According to MMT, we only get inflation when the economy expands very rapidly. So, why don't we just give people enough money so they don't have to work, but not too much money so that the economy isn't growing too rapidly?

The fact that other countries do have inflation and the fact that the US has not embarked on any of the spending projects listed above, such as eliminating all taxes, indicates that investors, economists, and government officials may not be fully convinced we can print endless money and never get inflation.

Perhaps more accurately, they are *hoping* that the lack of inflation so far will somehow manage to continue indefinitely. Perhaps they don't fully believe we have won our all-in bet that inflation will never happen. Perhaps investors, economists, and government officials are more concerned about eventually losing this all-in bet than they let on?

Fear and gambling, after all, are not so distant cousins.

The Real Reason Why We Have No Inflation Yet – It's Also Not What You May Think

The answer to the question "Why hasn't inflation happened yet?" has a very simple answer, but it's very hard to see because it has a lot to do with something economics typically ignores: *Psychology.*

Please take a moment to consider this new way of looking at inflation. You need to understand this if you want to protect yourself and grow real wealth in the dangerous times ahead.

We have no significant inflation yet, even after a decade of massive money printing, because businesses have not yet *decided* to significantly raise prices. Massive money printing, on its own, is not enough to create inflation. **Inflation requires BOTH money printing AND businesses deciding to raise prices.**

The idea that business owners have to *decide to raise prices* in order to get inflation comes as a big surprise to most people. Most of us have been led to believe that money printing alone causes inflation (typically in about 18–24 months), when in fact money printing is only half of the story.

The other half of the inflation story is that *businesses must decide to raise their prices.* Higher prices are *not* automatically triggered. The government doesn't force businesses to raise prices. When massive money printing has occurred, real people (businesses owners) – not some abstract theoretical economic force – have to deliberately decide to raise or not raise their prices. If, and when, enough of them do so, inflation begins.

This means that massive money printing alone is not enough to cause inflation here or in any country. But the group psychology of business owners matters. A lot. In fact, group psychology is critically important to why we don't have significant inflation yet, despite 10+ years of massive money printing. And group psychology will be critically important to why we do get significant inflation in the future.

So instead of asking, "When will inflation start and why hasn't inflation happened yet?" the better question to ask is . . .

When Will Businesses Raise Prices, and Why Hasn't It Happened Yet?

Again, the answer is simple, but not immediately obvious: Businesses will raise prices when the current group psychology of business owners changes.

In a bubble economy, group psychology has a massive impact on asset values (stocks, bonds, real estate, oil, etc.) and also on *inflation*.

Currently, business and investor psychology is very anti-inflation. Both groups seem to know implicitly that inflation is the biggest threat to the government-stimulated economy and asset markets. They seem to know intuitively that the government's ability to print money – *without creating inflation* – is the key to the continued success of the bubble economy. Hence, they have implicitly and explicitly denied that money printing can cause inflation.

Can Group Psychology Actually Stop or Slow Inflation?

Absolutely!

Think about it: If businesses don't raise prices, how can you get inflation? Sure, the government may be printing money like crazy, but if businesses don't raise their prices, no inflation is created. Governments don't raise prices – they just print money. To get inflation as a result of money printing, it is up to businesses to raise prices. As long as businesses don't raise their prices, prices will not go up.

In general, businesses are making a very rational decision that the big Fake Money bubble economy is good for them. They want the government to be able to keep stimulating the economy and pushing up asset prices. Losing a little revenue by not raising prices is a small price to pay for an incredible, unbelievable economy that is always expanding.

Investors Are Part of This Group Psychology, Too

If businesses don't raise prices, it's easy for investors to also think that there is little risk of significant long-lasting inflation. Hence, they are quite willing to lose a little money to inflation, or even lose a little money investing in negative-interest rate bonds that pay far less than inflation. Why? Because doing so helps to keep the whole bubble economy afloat and asset prices (such as stocks and real estate) soaring.

Just like businesses owners, investors are making a very rational decision. Losing a little money on low-interest-rate long-term bonds is meaningless compared to the massive profits to be made in a bubble stock market and a bubble real estate market.

Also, when interest rates fall, even the value of bonds, not just stocks and real estate, goes up. So, the actual pain of low interest rates due to low inflation doesn't affect older bonds that were issued earlier at higher interest rates – it actually makes them more valuable. Only when interest rates rise due to inflation does it make the bonds bought earlier worth less. And, so far, that hasn't happened, even though inflation is rising.

Until now, the modern industrial US economy has never experienced the enormous influence of group psychology on inflation. That's because we've never had a massive bubble economy that so desperately needed massive government stimulus (Fake Money) to survive.

In a non-bubble economy, massive money printing would definitely be a significant negative for businesses and investors. But now, for our modern advanced industrial economy and others, massive money printing has become a TOTAL POSITIVE. Party on, Garth!

"And this is where we adjust the interest rate."

Economics Needs to Revolutionize Its Theory of Inflation

Classic economic theory says that money printing causes inflation. As Nobel Prize–winning economist Milton Friedman famously said, "Inflation is always and everywhere a monetary phenomenon."

The authors of this book used to agree with that. In fact, our previous books quoted Friedman several times. We also highlighted excerpts from research by the Federal Reserve Bank of Minneapolis showing that inflation consistently follows the expansion of the money supply in a one-to-one correlation, regardless of the measure of money supply used.

Our previous books also discussed traditional factors affecting inflation, such as the velocity of money and the multiplier effect of bank lending. We also discussed how the typical delay for inflation after money printing (lag factor) is usually about 18–24 months.

But none of this is sufficient to explain the onset of inflation, because it is only half the story. Without the other half of the story kicking in, significant inflation simply doesn't begin.

So instead of saying that "Inflation is always and everywhere a monetary phenomenon," we need to revolutionize our concept of inflation creation by saying . . .

Inflation Is Always and Everywhere a Function of Businesses Raising Prices

Classical economic theory on inflation has to be modified to see that the onset of inflation is more than a simple economic output created by a simple economic input, as if getting inflation is like passively getting an illness.

Inflation is not a disease caused by money printing. We don't catch it after doing something wrong (i.e., printing too much money), even though many economists and Wall Street analysts think of it in those terms.

Instead, the onset of inflation is the result of human behavior. And human behavior is a choice made by many individual people, not an automatic cause-and-effect condition.

In fact, businesses can choose to avoid inflation – if enough of them individually make that choice. If businesses together decide not to raise prices too much, we simply do not get significant inflation.

It's simple, but also true. We don't need long scholarly articles or complex dissertations to prove it. It's an obvious fact.

Even After Massive Money Printing, If Businesses Don't Raise Prices Much, We Won't Get Significant Inflation

This is true no matter how much money we print. For example, if the government increases the money supply by 1000% and businesses raise their prices by 5%, inflation will be 5%. Period.

Yes, printing money is the basis for all inflation. And, yes, additional economic factors, such as monetary velocity and the multiplier effect, also affect the rate of inflation. But while those conditions are necessary, *they are not sufficient.* One other key factor must occur for inflation to begin: businesses must willingly raise prices. If businesses chose not to raise prices significantly, there will be no significant inflation – by definition.

In the past, the willingness of businesses to raise prices has always been a factor in creating inflation; it just wasn't very important. The reason it wasn't very important in the past is that businesses always used to raise prices, whether those businesses were in the US, England, Turkey, or Argentina. Money was printed, business raised prices, and inflation went up. Again, if businesses did not raise prices, we wouldn't have gotten any inflation at all.

Today, many businesses are raising their prices somewhat, but not that much and not that fast – certainly, not as fast as we are printing money! In the last 14 years, the US has increased the money supply by a stunning 1000%. But is inflation up anywhere near 1000%? Absolutely not. Why not? Because businesses did not raise their prices 1000%. You really cannot argue with this. It's simply a fact.

Once you take a moment to think about it, this new way of understanding inflation is quite obvious, yet it is entirely contrary to what the Federal Reserve and almost all economists would predict.

What Is Stopping Businesses from Raising Prices Now, for the First Time in Modern History?

Yes, some prices have gone up during the pandemic. But, for the first time in modern economic history, businesses have not been raising prices at nearly the same rate as we are printing money for the last 10 years.

Why not?

Maybe it's because we are in the midst of the most massive worldwide bubble economy in history?

Maybe it's because each business owner – without necessarily discussing it with others or even consciously thinking about it – has come to their own similar conclusions that raising their prices significantly right now would be a very bad idea. Maybe without thinking too much about it, they nonetheless know there's a big Fake Money bubble on the line.

Keeping the Fake Money bubble going is in everyone's individual best interest. It's group psychology without having to convince the group. Each individual is getting it done.

What Will Trigger High, Long-Lasting Inflation?

Given that rising inflation takes *both* money printing *and* businesses raising prices and given that we have increased the money supply by a mindboggling 1000% since the Financial Crisis, it seems clear that the only thing keeping inflation at bay is the *collective group psychology* of many individual business owners.

Therefore, the only way we can get significant future inflation is if there is a significant change in group psychology among business owners and investors. As long as most businesses and investors are substantially benefiting from the bubble, don't expect the general anti-inflation mentality to change. And even if it starts to change a bit, it will take time for the anti-inflation mentality to fully collapse. That's because the anti-inflation mentality works. It helps the bubble economy prosper and asset prices (stocks and real estate) to continue to rise.

So, how can the stock market fall if everybody has an anti-inflation mentality?

Well, it takes a while. But eventually, it will fall. It happens to all bubbles. The bubble lives on and on, until it eventually goes too far, gets out of hand, and then some triggering event – even a seemingly minor triggering event – suddenly hits the economy and the bubble can't survive the pressure.

That triggering event could easily be the longer-term consequences of the Covid pandemic. Constraints on supply combined with increased demand stimulated by massive government giveaways may kick off an inflationary spiral. Also, businesses have started raising prices – in part to deal with losses during Covid – thus changing some of the anti-inflation mentality. They may even feel they must raise prices in order to survive.

Some business owners could also increasingly feel they are not benefiting as much from the Fake Money bubble as they used to. Once they start to feel that way, they will likely become more willing to raise prices. This is already starting to happen on a relatively small scale. But it may take a while to become significant.

As prices rise a bit, more business owners are more likely to join in. Businesses must buy from other businesses, and they will have little choice but to raise prices when their suppliers charge more. Or, when their employees demand higher wages.

Gradually, over time, prices move up. At some point, the group psychological calculus will begin to significantly shift. Businesses will start to believe that they will gain more by raising their prices than they will lose. On an individual basis, that will be true.

And that is when significant long-lasting inflation begins.

Understanding inflation is that simple and direct. No PhD required. Money printing PLUS businesses raising prices eventually cause inflation. In time, as the payoff of supporting the bubble declines, prices will rise, and significant inflation – or more accurately, stagflation, will begin.

It really is that simple. Any other explanation is just grasping at straws in order to justify *our nonrefundable all-in bet* that inflation will never occur.

By the Way, Modern Economic Theory Is Pure Fantasy

The idea that somehow "it's different this time" and now we can massively print and borrow money endlessly with no negative consequences is pure fantasy.

Instead of Modern Monetary Theory, we should rename it Modern Economic Fantasy Theory (MEFT). MEFT assumes that the laws of normal economics do not apply in a bubble economy. And it's true! As long as the bubble doesn't pop. MEFT has been carefully crafted to keep people believing it will never pop, thus ensuring that our wonderful big Fake Money bubble will live forever!

So don't be a buzz-killer (or a bubble killer). Step right up, Ladies and Gentlemen, and enjoy (while you can) the *Four Basic Tenets of Modern Economic Fantasy Theory:*

1. There's no free lunch, but there is plenty of free Fake Money!
2. Tomorrow's stock market will look a lot like today's stock market, only better!
3. Up is good, down is bad. That's why the market only goes up! (Also, because we won't let it go down.)
4. Anyone silly enough to think that massive government borrowing and massive money printing is a bad idea should go find a smart Ivy League economist to straighten them out. (You know, they were so good at warning us before the 2008 global Financial Crisis. Oh wait, never mind.)

There is an important reason why some otherwise intelligent people believe in such nonsense as Modern Economic Fantasy Theory, and why otherwise intelligent investors continue to believe we will never get significant long-lasting inflation. Sadly, we are all caught, not between a rock and a hard place, but between a fantasy and a hard place.

Fantasy, as you will see in Chapter 4, is a whole lot easier to accept.

Won't the Pandemic Stimulus End and Solve This Whole Fake Money Problem?

Yes, the pandemic, along with the pandemic stimulus, will end. But massive money printing and borrowing will not.

If you are wondering when and how we will stop the massive government stimulus, the unfortunate answer is we won't, because we can't. As explained in Chapter 2, long before the Covid Crisis, our economy was already completely dependent on massive government borrowing for its entire growth. Again, *all* of our economic growth since 2008 has been due to massive government borrowing. Without that borrowing, the economy would have fallen into a widespread recessionary-turned-depressionary spiral.

This will be even more true after the Covid Crisis. In the postpandemic economy, we theoretically should be able to reduce the amount of government borrowing as more people go back to work. But it is quite likely that we won't want to cut spending as much as we could. It's very tempting to spend free money.

For example, we could invest the "free" money into various projects, such as infrastructure, education, better childcare, a better military, and so on. Although they may be called investments, the reality is that few of these "investments" will be paid back in terms of higher tax revenues. Tax revenues may be raised to help pay for some of this spending. But more likely, most of the money will come from more borrowing from what is now seen as a nearly unlimited pot of free money.

So, while the need for pandemic stimulus will certainly decrease substantially over the next couple of years, don't expect to see deficits return to the $1 trillion level where they were before the pandemic. The need to massively print money to support deficits of $1.5–$2 trillion will likely remain long after the pandemic is over.

The alternative is bleak. The immediate consequences of ending or greatly reducing the flow of more and more Fake Money (massive money printing and spending) would be far worse than merely returning to life before the Covid Crisis or even to life before the 2008 Financial Crisis. That's because, as we saw in Chapter 2, we already had a bubble-based economy long before all that.

The immediate consequences of killing the continuous flow of Fake Money would be the death of most of our fake wealth.

In other words, the bubble will pop.

Between a Rock and Fantasyland

OK, so if we want any economic growth at all, we can't stop massive money borrowing. And, hence, we can't stop massive money printing. Also, we may want to keep printing to keep overvalued stock and real estate prices high. If asset prices fall dramatically, so will the economy. Whichever way you look at it, we will hit a rock the size of Gibraltar if we significantly reduce our massive borrowing and printing.

So, what do we do? *Move to Fantasyland!*

Instead of facing the obvious fact that lots of borrowing and printing is bad, we can move to Fantasyland and convince ourselves that we never have to pay it back. That way, borrowing all we want is simply not the problem it used to be. And as long as we are already living in Fantasyland, we might as well also feel confident that – for the first time in history – massive money printing money will *never* cause inflation.

Wow! Free money! Living in Fantasyland is so much easier and more comfortable than reality. Plus, those living in Fantasyland can prove that it's no fantasy! Just look at the last decade! So far, so good, despite tons of borrowing and tons of money printing.

And for anyone who is silly enough to think that the future consequences of borrowing and money printing will be like the past, just ask most Harvard-trained and other Ivy League economists. They will assure you that the future will certainly be like the past.

The best of the best have been living in Fantasyland for years, and they are more than happy to show you around. Nothing to worry about. It's all just great!

Won't Rising Inflation Bring Reality to Fantasyland?

You would think so, but not for a while.

Sure, some investors fear that inflation will push up interest rates. But that is unlikely to evict us from Fantasyland anytime soon. Even if interest rates do rise a bit in the near term, they are unlikely to go up enough to badly hurt the stock market.

The pandemic Fake Money stimulus has been rocketing up that already highly overvalued stock market even higher. What happens if a highly overvalued stock market hits a big speed bump, like a significant increase in interest rates? That won't just "correct" the market, it will start to collapse it.

That's why the Fed will be almost entirely focused on *keeping interest rates low* to support high stock and real estate prices. If they raise interest rates, even if it is done in order to fight inflation, the market will react poorly. And, if the market reacts very poorly, the Fed will quickly decide that high interest rates aren't that necessary after all, and right back to Fantasyland we shall go, regardless of the early stages of rising inflation.

The Fed has shown great sensitivity in the last couple years to supporting the stock market, and there's no reason for them to change now. They must support it. Even in 2019, when the economy was doing just fine, the Fed stopped raising rates because it was negatively affecting the stock market. Nothing is more important to the Fed than supporting the stock market.

> You saw the reaction in the markets when the Fed just even hinted at tightening. I don't think they can tighten a lot without having a big, negative effect.
> — *Ray Dalio, founder of Bridgewater Associates,*
> *the world's largest hedge fund*

Also, any real attempt to fight inflation will require more than a 1% or 2% increase in interest rates. To reduce inflation, much larger interest rate hikes will be needed, and that is something the Fed wants to avoid at all costs. Hence, if the government has trouble selling its bonds at 2% when inflation is 5%, expect the Fed to simply buy those bonds the Treasury can't sell. If inflation hits 8%, expect the Fed to buy more bonds that the Treasury can't sell at 2%.

So, instead of raising interest rates to fight inflation, the Fed will fight higher interest rates by allowing inflation to rise. And they are making the right choice for the stock market, real estate market, and the economy. An increase in interest rates to 5%, 8%, or 10% would devastate the markets and the economy. Whereas inflation of 5%, 8%, or 10% – without high interest rates – won't hurt markets or the economy nearly as much. In some ways, inflation could even help.

So, the Fed's response to higher inflation in the future will be simple: Print more and more money! Buy more bonds to keep interest rates low. And at all costs, keep the economy and markets from collapsing.

Will that be a problem in the longer term? Absolutely! But the government and Wall Street don't think too much about the future; they worry about avoiding an immediate collapse. That makes sense . . . sort of. Nobody likes a collapse. The Fed certainly is not going to purposely trigger it by greatly reducing or ending massive money printing. And neither will Congress greatly reduce or end massive borrowing.

This Market Can't Handle the Truth

Have you noticed how good news is good for the stock market and how bad news is also good for the stock market?

Every time another piece of bad news comes out about slow job creation or rising inflation, the market takes a short little hit and then quickly shrugs it off. It's a Teflon market, right?

No, it's actually more than that. This market cannot handle the truth about the economy, inflation, or the massive stimulation being gifted to the market by the government. The more overvalued the market, the more vulnerable it becomes to the risk of facing the truth rationally without causing a major collapse. Hence, it simply treats bad news as irrelevant or as simply wrong.

Also, if you look more closely, the market is smarter than you think in some ways. It is actively trying to cover up bad news. It knows very well what's bad news, and it goes up to minimize that bad news to make the US and our economy look better.

Stock market investors are cheerleaders – not just for stocks but for the US as well. If something goes wrong, like the US having the worst Covid Crisis in the world on a per capita basis despite having the best health care system in the world and spending more than double on its health care system than any other industrialized nation, the market soars to record highs. The soaring market distracts us from an obvious negative.

You may think this sounds a like a big conspiracy theory. But it's not. This is an example of the power of group psychology – in this case, on the stock market. Just like the group psychology among business owners that has been keeping inflation low for the past 10 years, the group psychology among investors is keeping the vulnerable stock market bubble up.

For obvious reasons, investors want the US to look good to make it clear why our stock and real estate markets are booming. Any news that makes the US look bad must be ignored.

Even better, the market has decided to greet news that makes the US look bad as another reason to push the overvalued market up even further. Those rising stock and real estate markets make it easier to praise the US. How could the US be making big mistakes if its stock market and housing market are doing so well? We must be doing something right!

Sounds good. But the only reason the US economy is growing and the stock market and real estate markets are booming is that we are making a much bigger mistake than we have ever made before – at least economically. We are creating an enormous amount of Fake Money.

"Just when I'm beginning to lose faith in the economy, the market hits another all-time high."

Does Fantasyland Mean We're Headed for an Immediate Market Collapse? Not a Chance!

You might think that if delusion is keeping the market up, then it can all end quickly and suddenly when that delusion pops.

Surprisingly, no.

That's one of the benefits of having the government artificially support the markets. If the market is having problems, the government (both the Fed and Congress) can and will move quickly to support it – just as they did in March 2020 during the Covid Crisis. The Fed and Congress will do all they can to keep the markets going up for as long as they possibly can.

So, long before the final collapse (the Financial Cliff), the government will make numerous attempts to try to save the market. We won't hit the Financial Cliff overnight. It will happen in stages over a long lead-up period.

Nonetheless, almost no one will see it coming because they don't want to see it. Most investors will go right over the Cliff because they will continue to assume it will never happen or they think it will bounce back up and the downturn is just a great buying opportunity, as it has been in the past.

Will the Fed Buy Stocks to Keep Prices High?

Our earlier books said this was unlikely because, at that time, it would have scared the market.

But now that the market is deep in Fantasyland, what used to be scary may no longer be so concerning. The Fed quite possibly will decide to buy stocks if necessary to keep the market from collapsing.

Will investors like it? Absolutely!

The central banks of other countries are already doing it, most notably, the Bank of Japan, which buys stocks at regular intervals. Government intervention in the financial markets is more normal in the Japan than in the US, and it hasn't bothered Japanese stock investors so far.

Will it bother US stock market investors? Certainly, it will bother some market participants. But if the lack of concern over massive money printing and government borrowing is any indication, they won't worry about it too much. The market is less focused on fundamentals now than ever before. They simply want the market to go up, and, so far, they don't seem to care too much about why it goes up.

The level of stock analysis by most investors today is best summed up by the saying, "Up is good, down is bad." Who needs to think any deeper than that?

Of course, because Fantasyland is not real and therefore cannot last, all the money printing done to buy stocks and bonds, and to fund government deficits will eventually create significant rising inflation. Over time, as inflations goes higher and higher, the markets will react increasingly poorly to more and more money printing for whatever reason – even to buy stocks.

Desperately Seeing Normalcy

Some stock market investors are desperately hoping we have a normal stock market. In particular, they want a stock market that corrects when it is overvalued. Corrections and bear markets are both actually signs of a healthy market. More importantly, it indicates a normal, non-manipulated market.

A market that has very few corrections looks abnormal and very much like a manipulated market. Right now, we have a market that makes very few corrections. That's why more than a few investment analysts and hedge fund managers are warning that this market is overvalued and due for a correction, perhaps a very big correction.

Although a big correction in the near term is possible, it's unlikely. A highly overvalued market, like the one we have today, can easily go from a correction (10% decline) to a bear market (20% decline) to a collapse. Therefore, the best way for the market to prevent a collapse is to have very few corrections and no bear markets – at least none that last for very long.

So, market psychology is very oriented toward what has always been true to some extent but has now become a necessity: Up is good, down is bad. Of course, a very stock-market-supportive Congress and Fed that are willing to borrow massively and print money massively are the ultimate backstop to this "up is good, down is bad" market psychology.

Although Congress, the president, and the Fed don't say directly that they are trying to support the stock market, their actions are clearly very supportive of keeping the market going up. They know a collapsing stock market would quickly lead to a collapsing economy. So, even if their focus is on artificially boosting the economy, the effect of their policies is also to artificially boost the stock market.

So, relax when some pundits or money managers tell you a big correction/bear market is about to hit. They mostly just want to distract you, and themselves, from the fact that this market is heavily manipulated and artificially stimulated. The more they assume the market is normal and not being artificially manipulated, the better they make themselves, and you, feel about the market in the long term.

It's just not reality. This market is about as far from normal as it has ever been. It will continue to be so until we hit the Financial Cliff and the big Fake Money bubble pops.

What If We Start Cutting Deficit Spending Now?

What if we could get together a bipartisan group of people in Congress who would be ready to cut spending by $100 billion annually? That would be a huge cut, almost five times NASA's entire budget. It's never been done before, but what if we could somehow get it done? Wouldn't that help?

Unfortunately, it wouldn't matter a damn.

Why? Because our current federal deficit is over $2 trillion and our total federal debt is more than $30 trillion. Cutting the current $2 trillion deficit to $1.9 trillion is meaningless. That's part of the reason there is a lot less interest in cutting the deficit these days, even among fiscal conservatives. The deficit is already so big, it just doesn't matter anymore. Even the most painful cuts (which would be very damaging to the economy) would have no impact on our $30 trillion total debt. It's still going to keep rising at an incredibly fast pace.

The same is true for money printing. If we had only increased our money supply from the $800 billion in 2007 by

$100 billion, then reducing our money supply by $50 billion would make a big difference.

But instead, we increased our money supply from $800 billion in 2007 to *$8 trillion*. Reducing this by $50 billion is meaningless. And we are adding more and more, printing over $100 billion per month in early 2021. That means a $50 billion reduction in our money supply would be erased in just *two weeks*. Any serious reduction in our money supply, and even at the rate we are increasing it, is hopeless. Not going to happen.

The Fed may talk about reducing money printing ("tapering"), and they might even do a bit of that. But only for show. Big cuts, whether it's equal to the amount of money we are borrowing or the amount of money we are printing, could happen. But at this point, it just wouldn't matter a damn.

Fake Money . . . Real Support

There is real danger ahead, and we all need to prepare for what will likely be a devastating blow to investments, livelihoods, and wealth.

For the latest updates as we approach the inevitable Financial Cliff and Aftershock ahead, please visit www.fakemoneyrealdanger.com or www.aftershockpublishing.com.

There you can also sign up to receive any of our email alert services – *all 100% free.*

Or contact us at 703-787-0139 or info@aftershockpublishing.com.

For private consulting for individuals, businesses, and groups, please contact *Fake Money, Real Danger* and *Aftershock* coauthor Cindy Spitzer at 443-980-7367 or information@arksma.com Your first call is free.

For hands-on investment management based on the macroeconomic views and investment strategies described in our books, please contact Ark Financial Management at 703-774-3520, 888-238-8370 or information@arksma.com.

5

How to Make the Most Money Now – First, Avoid Picking Individual Stocks Despite Enormous Pressure to Do So

Picking the right stocks that will beat the overall market averages has never been easy. In fact, long before the 2008 Financial Crisis, and even before the current stock market boom that started in the 1980s, a man named John Bogle saw just how hard it was to pick stocks that would outperform the market indexes. In fact, very few stock-picking mutual fund managers were able to beat the market, despite charging big fees for their stock-picking skills.

John Bogle had a better idea. Instead of trying to be a better stock picker, Mr. Bogle decided the way to beat 'em was to join 'em, so to speak. Hence, in 1976 he created the first stock index fund.

The company he founded, The Vanguard Company, offered the first index fund available to the general public. It was appropriately named, the First Index Investment Trust, which was basically an index fund for the S&P 500.

Based on his research, Mr. Bogle made a bet that an index fund with low fees could outperform most actively managed mutual funds, containing hand-picked stocks, over the long term. He was right. And over time he was proven even more correct. Study after study has shown that actively managed stock-picking funds consistently fail to outperform the broader market as whole.

In other words, don't waste your money paying experts to pick individual stocks that might beat the market: choose the whole market instead, and you will beat the active managers.

This concept has proven true time and again. For example, in 2019, the Standard & Poor's Dow Jones Indices reported that after 10 years, 85% of actively managed large cap funds *underperformed* the S&P 500. And after 15 years, nearly 92% of actively managed large cap funds were trailing behind the index. While it is true that some managers may outperform the S&P 500 for a year or two, they almost never outperform the S&P over 10–15 years as shown in Figure 5.1.

The Vanguard Company and its family of index funds eventually grew to become the largest provider of mutual funds in the world. Proof positive that good ideas can win in the end, even if at first they are unpopular among potential customers and the rest of the industry. Vanguard has more than $5.3 trillion under management, although not all of that is in index funds.

In August 2019, assets held in index funds overtook actively managed funds. Index funds held $4.27 trillion in assets surpassing actively managed funds, which held $4.24 trillion.

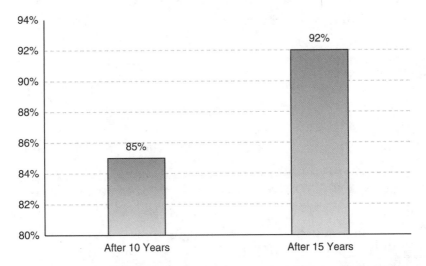

Figure 5.1   In 2019 the Vast Majority of Actively Managed Large-Cap Stock Mutual Funds Trailed the S&P 500 Over Both a 10-Year and 15-Year Period

Source: Standard and Poor's Dow Jones Indices.

Between 2009 and 2019, 85% of actively managed large cap funds underperformed the S&P 500. Between 2004 and 2019 nearly 92% trailed the S&P 500.

Since the Financial Crisis, Beating the Market with Stock Picking Has Become Almost Impossible

Market-beating stock picking has always been hard to do. However, in a stock bubble like the one we have been in since the Financial Crisis, stock picking is even more difficult than it was in the 1960s or 1970s. In fact, it's been almost impossible, even for the best stock pickers.

For example, Warren Buffett, certainly one of the best stock pickers of the last 50 years, has been unable to beat the most recent incarnation of the bubble stock market, trailing the S&P 500 average since 2008. He just can't find stocks that are undervalued. Normal value investing analysis doesn't work when everything is overvalued. Sure, some stocks are less highly overvalued than others, but they are *almost all overvalued.*

Supposedly, the best stock pickers of all are the billionaire hedge fund managers who are often paid more than a billion dollars a year because they are so good at picking stocks that beat the market. Interestingly, Warren Buffett was so annoyed by many hedge fund managers' claims of beating the market that he put them to a test. It was called the Buffett challenge.

In 2008, he publicly challenged the hedge fund industry by wagering $500,000 that no investment professional could select a set of at least five hedge funds that would, over a 10-year period, match the performance of the S&P 500, after deducting the hedge funds' fees.

Ted Seides of Protégé Partners LLC accepted the bet. He chose five groups of hedge funds. These groups of funds were what's called a fund of funds. Each fund held limited partnerships in a group of hedge funds. By picking five groups of funds, instead of just five funds, Mr. Seides distributed his risk among many of what he considered to be the best hedge funds in the industry.

Each of the five fund of funds is shown in Figure 5.2 below. During the course of the wager, *none* of the fund of funds beat the S&P 500. In fact, only one fund came close. The other four performed miserably compared to the S&P 500. They all made money, but *none* beat the S&P 500 index. The broader hedge fund index also failed to come close to the performance of the S&P 500.

What's even more interesting than the miserable performance of the hedge fund billionaires is that a simple group of zero-coupon Treasury bonds blew away both the hedge funds' performance AND the S&P 500. The simplest and "dumbest" investment of all turned out to be the best performer. The basket of zero couple bonds was chosen by Mr. Buffett and Mr. Seides as a good safe place to invest the money they were betting in 2008.

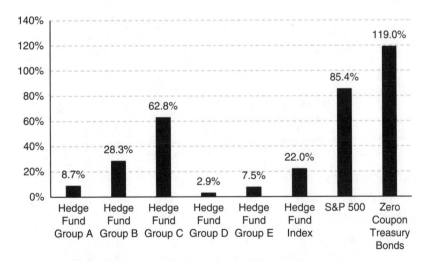

Figure 5.2 The Performance of the Various Investments during the Buffett Challenge

Source: Berkshire Hathaway's 2016 Letter to Shareholders.

None of the five groups of hedge funds in the Buffett Challenge beat the S&P 500. However, a simple "dumb" investment in zero coupon bonds did. Not a great performance for the best stock pickers in the world.

One caveat: The bonds were actually redeemed in February 2015, so their performance is only through 2015 and not the full 10 years.

As mentioned earlier, mutual fund managers have also not been able to beat the market. In the 10 years from 2009 to 2019, 85% of large cap mutual fund managers failed to even match, never mind beat, the performance of the S&P 500. The post-financial crisis stock bubble has been a really tough time for stock pickers.

As a further example, let's take a look at Warren Buffett himself. He is certainly one of the greatest stock pickers of all time. His investment vehicle, Berkshire Hathaway, has also been unable to beat the S&P 500, as shown in Figure 5.3.

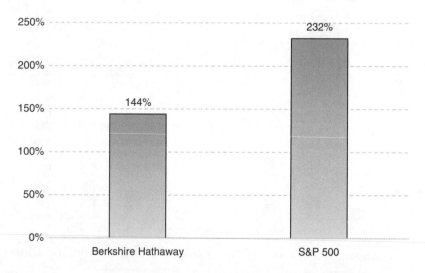

Figure 5.3   Warren Buffett's Performance Compared to the S&P 500 from June 1, 2012 to August 2, 2020

Source: Standard & Poor's.

Warren Buffett's investment vehicle, Berkshire Hathaway, has struggled to beat the S&P 500 in the last decade despite Mr. Buffett being one of the best stock pickers of all time.

Stock pickers like Warren Buffett don't do so well in a bubble largely because the longer the bubble lasts the more likely most assets have become highly correlated, as is increasingly the case today. Assets that go up together also tend to go down together. Also, as all stocks become overpriced, it becomes increasingly difficult to find a good value to buy.

Stock picking simply doesn't work in a long-standing bubble. Of course, in a falling bubble, stock picking doesn't help, either. Picking a different seat on the boat as it heads over a waterfall is not a great way to reduce risk.

And it's not just great stock pickers like Warren Buffett who are having trouble beating the market. Famous hedge fund managers like Bill Ackman are having even more trouble. Although hedge fund managers invest in more than just public stocks for their funds, they are considered great stock pickers since that is often the majority of assets they hold. However, stock picking has proved difficult for even the most celebrated hedge fund managers. As Figure 5.4 shows, Mr. Ackman's Pershing Square Capital fund hasn't even come close to beating the S&P 500 in the last 10 years.

Bill Ackman may not manage the largest hedge fund in the world, but Ray Dalio does. His fund, Bridgewater Associates, manages over $150 billion. He is certainly one of the best hedge fund managers in the business and one of the best stock pickers out there.

So has the biggest done the best? Not at all.

In fact, Dalio's performance is only slightly better than Ackman's, trailing the S&P 500 by 65% as shown in Figure 5.5. Again, you would be much better off putting your money in a low-cost Vanguard S&P 500 index fund.

We aren't pointing out the poor performance of Warren Buffett, Bill Ackman, and Ray Dalio to pick on them. They are

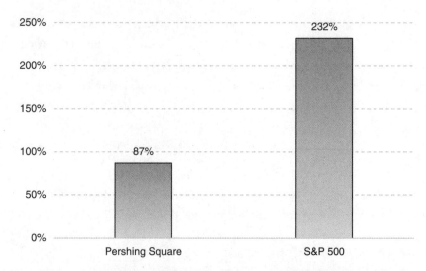

Figure 5.4   Performance of Billionaire Hedge Fund Manager Bill Ackman's Pershing Square Capital Fund Compared to the S&P 500 from June 1, 2012 to August 2, 2021

Source: TipRanks, Standard & Poor's.

Bill Ackman doesn't manage the biggest hedge fund in the world, but he is in the business news a lot. His financial engineering of stock purchases is considered some of the best in the industry. However, his performance doesn't show great financial engineering. In fact, he trails the S&P 500 by a whopping 145%. So, if you had simply put your money into a low-cost Vanguard index fund, you would have beaten one of the most acclaimed hedge fund managers in the business. And you wouldn't have had to pay him the multibillion-dollar fees that made him a billionaire.

top-notch investors and stock pickers. **The point is that even the best of the best stock pickers fails to beat the market. In fact, they miss by a long shot.**

Very few money managers who pick stocks are likely to do any better than these "best of the best" investment managers. Yet almost any money manager who simply buys stocks or index funds that follow the S&P 500 will beat them. Not because that manager is any better at investing than these people, but because it's almost impossible to analyze and value stocks in a bubble market that is so out of touch with

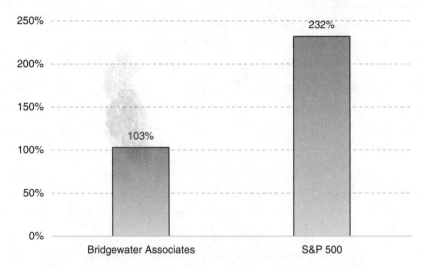

Figure 5.5   Performance of the World's Largest Hedge Fund, Bridgewater Associates, Compared to the S&P 500 from June, 1 2012 to August 2, 2021
Source: TipRanks, Standard & Poor's.
Bridgewater Associates trails the S&P 500 by almost 130% in the last decade.

reality, as this market has increasingly become since the Financial Crisis.

This is one time where taking the easy route will do much better than the difficult route – that is, until we get high inflation. Then it will get extremely tough for everyone.

If Stock Picking Doesn't Work, Why Do Investors Focus on It So Much?

The short answer is because, at one time, stock picking was a source of growth for stock investments.

Understanding how this occurred takes a bit of a longer answer. To understand why stock picking became so important, let's take a brief look at its history.

Believe it or not, stock picking actually started with *bond picking*. The earliest seeds of today's deeply entrenched stock-picking mentality actually started a century ago with bonds and Moody's bond rating service.

John Moody is considered the inventor of modern bond credit ratings in the US. His first publication, in 1900, was *Moody's Manual of Industrial and Miscellaneous Securities.* He provided detailed information and statistics on a wide variety stocks and bonds. Unfortunately, Mr. Moody went bankrupt in the 1907 financial crisis. However, not one to give up easily, he started publishing again in 1909 with an analysis of railroads, titled appropriately, *Analysis of Railroad Investments.*

In 1913, Mr. Moody published his first *Moody's Manual,* which actually offered ratings of public securities using a letter rating system. In 1913, he changed the name to Moody's Investor Services, which is the modern Moody's we know today. Other rating companies followed him with Poor's in 1916, Standard Statistics Company in 1922, and the Fitch Publishing Company in 1924.

By 1924, Moody's was rating nearly the entire US bond market. These bond ratings were a huge step forward in analyzing the riskiness of investing in a bond. It was the beginning of true security analysis. Before that, investors in public company debt simply had to rely on what companies told them or what some of their friends told them. With Moody's they could get an unbiased third-party analysis (the subscriber paid for the reports, not the company) and make an informed and properly analyzed investment decision based on the fundamental (and real) conditions of the company.

Thus, Moody's and its competitors were the beginning of well-researched bond picking, which, of course, eventually led to well-researched stock picking based on good fundamental analysis by trained professionals. Stock and bond investing became a lot less like gambling on a horse and much more like a real investment decision.

Stock picking helped give the stock market the fundamental support it needed to attract more investors. Government regulations of the market, adopted in the 1930s, also helped give investors more confidence that the market was honest. It also forced more disclosure of a company's fundamentals to both stock investors and stock analysts, like Moody's. Broader and more honest disclosure made stock picking an even more powerful tool for finding the best investments.

Enter the Modern Stock Picker, Merrill Lynch, and the Beginning of the Stock Investment Industry

Merrill Lynch introduced America to stocks in the 1950s. The time was right. The post–World War II boom had led to dramatic increases in income and savings. People needed some place to put those savings that would hopefully give them a higher return than a savings account.

With a rapidly booming economy, there were opportunities, but people were still fearful of stocks after the stock market crash of the Great Depression. Sure, stocks had recovered all their losses by 1937, but the psychological damage remained. Stocks were still viewed as risky in the 1950s, and investors needed someone to help them minimize that risk while still fetching a higher return than bonds.

At Merrill Lynch, stock analysts performed this valuable function by helping stock salesman find stocks that would perform well and were a good fit for certain investors. They provided an important service in helping to sell what was an important new product – stocks that were good investments for retail investors and not just gamblers. They helped produce the modern 60/40 portfolio of 60% stocks, chosen for a particular investor's risk level, and 40% highly rated bonds for secure income with limited risk of capital loss.

Unfortunately, most stock analysts employed by stock brokerage firms and underwriters eventually just became stock cheerleaders and stock salespeople for the stock market bubble. By the 1990s, over 90% of stocks were rated as "buys" or "holds." Very few "sell" recommendations were issued.

After the dot-com crash in 2000, the same was true. Analysts were really just stock salesman. Mark Mayo, an excellent banking stock analyst wrote a book, *Exile on Wall Street: One Analyst's Fight to Save the Big Banks from Themselves*, on the pressure he felt to rate banking stocks highly before the Financial Crisis of 2008.

Not that much changed after the Financial Crisis. Although there were modest changes in ethical standards for stock analysts, the reality is that stock analysts still rate 85–90% of all stocks as buys or holds.

Stock analysts for big brokerage firms were becoming more like stock cheerleaders in the 1980s and 1990s, but stock picking was just hitting its peak after a lull in the inflation-racked 1970s.

Stock Picking Peaked in the 1980s

Nobody embodies the 1980s stock-picking boom better than Peter Lynch. Lynch ran the Magellan Fund for Fidelity Investments. Between 1977 and 1990, the Magellan Fund averaged a 29.2% annual return as shown in Figure 5.6, handily beating

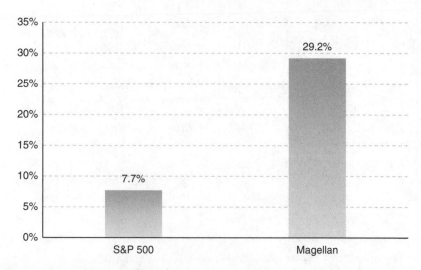

Figure 5.6 Average Annual Return for S&P 500 vs. Fidelity Magellan Fund Between 1977 and 1990

Source: Standard and Poor's, Fidelity Investments.

Peter Lynch, who managed Fidelity's Magellan fund from 1977 to 1990, set the gold standard for magnificent stock picking at a mutual fund.

the S&P 500, and making it the best-performing mutual fund in the world. His total assets under management grew from $18 million to $14 billion, at a time when a billion dollars under management was a lot.

It was no accident that he worked for Fidelity Investments. Fidelity helped pioneer the modern mutual fund industry by creating funds run by star managers like Peter Lynch, and it also created funds focusing on industry sectors (healthcare, utilities, consumer goods, etc.), market sectors (small caps, high growth stocks, high dividend stocks, etc.).

By the end of the 1990s, there were more publicly listed mutual funds than there were publicly listed stocks.

Fidelity Investments: Creating the Mutual Fund Industry

The Fidelity Fund was established in 1930. The fund operated through the Great Depression until 1943 when Boston-based lawyer Edward C. Johnson II acquired it. Assets under management were $3 million.

In the early 1950s, Fidelity hired Gerry Tsai, a young immigrant from Shanghai, China, to help run the Fidelity Fund as a stock picker. Tsai started by buying speculative stocks like Xerox and Polaroid. His performance in the stock market gained him fame among investors, and in 10 years, the Fund's assets under management grew to over $1 billion.

In the 1960s and 1970s, Fidelity created a wide range of mutual funds focusing on industry sectors, types of stocks, such as growth stocks, small caps, or very high growth stocks. One of those funds was the Magellan Fund, founded in 1962 and was the highest-performing mutual fund in history.

In 1972, the markets were turbulent, and investors were moving to more secure investments. Fidelity Investments' mutual fund assets declined by 30% to $3 billion during the next two years. In response, Fidelity established the first retail money market fund, Fidelity Daily Income Trust (FIDIT).

The fund was also the first to offer check writing, and customers benefited from having the same liquidity as saving accounts, which was a massive change for an investment firm. What's amazing is that retail money market funds didn't even exist until 1972 – one more reason Fidelity is so important in the evolution of modern investing.

Another example of a star mutual fund manager was Bill Miller, who ran Legg Mason's Capital Management Value Trust. He beat the S&P 500 index for 15 consecutive years from 1991 through 2005. However, he had a rather spectacular collapse during the Financial Crisis by making big bets on housing-related stocks he thought were way undervalued.

In a way, Peter Lynch and Bill Miller bookended the glory days of stock pickers – Mr. Lynch helped start it and Mr. Miller helped finish it off.

No manager of the Magellan Fund after Lynch was able to match his record. However, the Fund grew from $18 billion when he left to more than $100 billion by 2000. Investments in mutual funds in the 1990s were increasing rapidly, even if performance was not.

"I don't get it—last time I jiggled the mouse this way we made a 16.45 per-cent profit."

Why Does Wall Street Desperately Want Stock Picking to Work?

Wall Street does not want to give up stock picking because it serves two very important functions for supporting the stock market bubble.

First, stock picking is a very good way for stock salespeople to get investors to buy stocks. Look at CNBC and the entire brokerage community. Look at all of the books and newsletters devoted to beating the market by hunting for future stock winners. Look at all the hyped-up IPOs for profitless companies. In order for stock salespeople to earn lots of money, they need to sell, sell, sell! Without promoting stock picking, the entire stock-selling industry would go under.

Second, and much more important, stock pickers MUST keep picking and buying stocks in order for the market to recover from declines. Without stock picking, a market decline could easily become a total collapse if the index funds were the only investors.

This is absolutely critical to the success of the market and to the support of the market bubble. A few people have pointed out the dangers from so-called *passive investing*. With over 50% of mutual fund investors in index or passive (no-conviction) investing, the pool of investors who will help the market recover from a decline is dwindling.

So far, the problems have been manageable and have resulted more in high volatility rather than a collapse. But as the pool of investors willing to help a market recover from a decline dwindles due to being burned or lack of conviction, the overwhelming size of the passive investing community will ultimately greatly accelerate the popping of the stock market bubble.

The Massive Stock Bubble Is Protecting Stock Pickers from Facing Poor Performance

As long as it keeps going up, a rising stock bubble protects stock pickers from having to face poor performance. In a rising bubble market, where all stocks are generally going up, stock picking is like being a gambler who owns the casino – *the odds are always on your side.* No matter what stocks you pick, the rising bubble makes sure that you will succeed to some extent.

Many people say they are great stock pickers, but very few have the record to prove it. That doesn't mean that some of them don't have legions of followers. Investors like stock pickers because following their advice makes them feel like they are doing something special rather than just investing in an index. And, hence, they will receive a big payoff, if not now, then later. It is something like having a special technique or insider secret to win at a casino. Investors also like hedge funds because it makes them feel special, despite bad returns.

Also, to be clear, some funds, especially in their formative years when their founders are hungry, have done very well. But it rarely lasts.

So stock pickers get to keep picking stocks without paying too high a price for continuing to support stock salespeople and continuing to support the stock bubble – at least until the bubble pops.

When the bubble pops, all stock pickers will plummet over the Financial Cliff. At that point, the best stock picking in the world won't save them.

However, until then, it is **very important to investors to keep the bubble going at all costs**. Stock pickers may say their goal is beating the market, but in fact, their real top priority is *saving the market*. That's why the market was able to do so well in 2020 when the economy was doing so poorly (see Appendix A).

It's all about saving the bubble.

Wait a Minute! I've Had Some Great Stock Picks!

Of course you have! And so have many other people. Many, many investors have had stock picks that crushed the S&P 500. So, obviously it can be done.

The problem is that it simply *cannot be done consistently for years and across an entire portfolio*. The best stock pickers in the world have proven that again and again.

The occasional hit of a good stock pick makes us want to keep trying for another hit. And even when we don't win, a near miss also is seductive: "If only I had bought more Apple stock I'd be a millionaire by now!" Of course, these are often very true statements.

And the fact that many people have had stock picks that did beat or crush the S&P 500 (or have come close) gives many investors – amateurs and professionals – the feeling that all they need to do is find the next big stock (Tesla, Apple, Uber, Facebook . . .) and just invest more heavily in them than they have done in the past when they were more cautious investors.

It's like being in Las Vegas and getting a couple of big wins, or just missing a big win, in a card game or at the roulette wheel. Every win and every near miss encourage you to try again. It's a mentality that can affect a lot of people because it seems to make so much sense.

Psychologists have studied this phenomenon in experiments with mice. "Intermittent reinforcement" – in which a mouse gets a wonderful reward for pushing a bar, like a hit of cocaine, but only gets it randomly – will make mice push that bar over and over and over again, even when the pay-off is very infrequent and even when the consequences of wasting time and energy on pushing the bar are great (like starvation).

In other words, getting an occasional hit is addictive.

We may not die of starvation like a mouse pushing a bar that randomly dispenses cocaine, but we do keep trying to beat the market with stock picking – even though it *absolutely does not work.*

What it does do is keep the stock market bubble afloat – at least for now.

Fashion Investing

A version of stock picking that has become extremely popular, post-Covid, is what we call "fashion investing." By that we don't mean investing in fashion. We mean investing in what's fashionable.

Investing in what is fashionable at the time has always been popular to some extent, but nothing like it is today. And it wasn't nearly as important to the investing world nor as detached from reality as it is today.

Investing in RCA and radio might have been fashionable in the 1920s, but these companies were also involved in truly big innovation. On the other hand, investing in Dogecoin or GameStop, pushing their price up 3000% in a few months, is totally different. They aren't amazing innovations, and their absurd price increases dwarf anything in past fashionable investments, like RCA in the 1920s or Xerox in the 1960s.

Dogecoin, a cryptocurrency that was all the rage and skyrocketing in spring 2021, was heavily dependent upon how Elon Musk spoke about it in his appearance on Saturday Night Live. As Musk was performing his skits, fashion investors were reporting he did a poor job and Dogecoin plummeted in value. Really? Is that anything but a pure fashion play?

Meme stocks are classic fashion stocks. Meme stocks are stocks that get a huge retail investor following and soar. Lately, an investment news site on the Internet called Wall Street Bets, has led the charge on a number of stocks, including GameStop, a large chain of stores that sells computer games, which soared for no reason at all from $3 to $300. It fell to $150 a share but that's still a massive increase from $3 a share which is where it had been for years.

In another example, barbeque grills were announced as the next big IPO fashion in July 2021, with two grill companies going public. *Really? Barbeque grills?*

Although not stocks, we would have to classify NFTs as another hot fashion investment. NFTs are Non-Fungible Tokens. We know. That means nothing. Essentially, they are digital art creations that cannot be replicated. The idea is that they are like a da Vinci painting. The supply is limited, and there are no new daVinci paintings being created. It is highly unlikely there will be a lasting market for NFTs and the prices of all collectibles, including NFTs, paintings, classic cars, and so on, will crash when the stock market crashes.

Of course, if fashion investing hit a few freakish stocks in a relatively small way, it's really only a sidenote to the massive stock bubble. But fashion investing has become much more significant, especially during the Covid Crisis. Fashion investments like Tesla made Elon Musk the richest person in the world. Other fashion investments like Bitcoin have pushed the value of cryptocurrencies to over $1.4 trillion in July 2021. And that's after Bitcoin fell 50%.

We can already hear your response to that last paragraph: Bitcoin and Tesla are very different from GameStop and Dogecoin and BBQ grills. These are true innovations.

But, in reality, they are not innovations. Bitcoin has yet to show much value as a currency. And if it keeps jumping up or down, 10% in a day sometimes, it never will. Tesla is just one of many electric vehicle producers. Electric vehicles have not made a profit yet for any manufacturer. No doubt they will someday for some manufacturers, but that is hardly enough to justify the kinds of valuations that Tesla and some other electric car companies are getting.

In the fashion investment world, everybody just agrees that electric cars will rule the future – very shortly. By 2030, every car in Europe will be electric, etc.

This fantasy talk sounds similar to when people say that you will be able to burn your driver license in 10 years because we will no longer need to drive cars. Self-driving vehicles will take over. And there will be no truck driving jobs in the future because self-driving trucks will take over.

Sorry, not gonna happen.

In fact, self-driving may go down as a total and complete failure. The jury is still out on that, but the outlook is pretty grim right now.

However, in the fashion investing world, real problems are brushed aside, and everybody just repeats the same mantra – self-driving will take over the automotive world. Electric vehicles will replace everything! Fashion investing has risen to an enormously important level in today's investment community.

Even if electric cars become a breakthrough technology like gas-powered cars, they don't deserve the kind of incredible support and stock valuations they are currently getting.

Ford Motor did not get highly valued until it was much more proven, its cars sold well, and it made a very good profit. Ford cars really were a revolution and really did revolutionize American society.

Everybody now looks for the next hot market – hydrogen, green investments, rotation into value stocks, rotation into huge tech stocks.

It's a key part of stock picking – just look for the next revolution to invest in, and you will be the next stock millionaire! Or billionaire! Especially if you are an amazing hedge fund manager, who, in reality, hasn't beaten the S&P 500 for the last 10 years.

When investing has become incredibly profitable because the stock bubble is exploding, fashion investing is a key part of what makes people think the bubble is real. You're investing in amazing innovations such as self-driving cars, crypto currencies, fintech, hydrogen power, battery power.

In reality, you're just investing in the next fashion play, which could be a great stock investment. Nobody looks at, or is even aware of, a company's real valuation when it comes to a fashion play. That lack of scrutiny is a huge benefit when you are trying to maintain a stock bubble.

Fashion companies have great stock performance, not because they are truly making big profits from big innovation, but because they are very good (or lucky) at being a very fashionable in an investment world that is increasingly focused on picking fashion over company profits. Profits are just another way to limit a stock's growth potential.

If you don't worry about company profits and focus on what's fashionable (what's hot) the sky's the limit for a stock's price!

What bubble billionaire could ask for anything more?!

OK, If I Can't Pick Stocks, How Do I Make Money in the Market – Preferably a Lot of It?

Well, it turns out we have something for that.

Onward to Chapter 6!

How to Beat the Market Now and Get Out Before the Bubble Pops Later

What if the stock market keeps going up and up?

Or, what if the market goes up for a while and then suddenly drops?

Or, on the other hand, what if the market does not go up much from here?

Or, what if it goes down significantly over the long term?

What if, what if, what if?

That's the problem with investing: *no one knows the future.* And now that we are in an enormous, vulnerable Fake Money bubble, including an enormous stock market bubble that will inevitably hit the Financial Cliff, not knowing the details of the future poses an even bigger problem.

What's going to happen, when will it happen, and what are we going to do about it? We need a plan for making gains now, before the Financial Cliff. And we definitely need a plan for protection later when the Financial Cliff causes asset values to evaporate.

As mentioned earlier in the book, protection from the Financial Cliff is a problem that *every investor* – including you – must solve. Most will not see it coming. If you are among the few who do, having a plan to deal with it is absolutely essential.

We Have a Plan: Forget Stock Picking, Use a Terrific Trading System, and Safely Beat the Market

When any bubble is rising (or when a non-bubble market is performing well), simply getting in and staying in with a buy-and-hold investment strategy makes good sense. But what if the great uptrend doesn't continue? How will you protect yourself when the Financial Cliff hits and Fake Money bubble pops?

Because none of us knows when that will occur, we can't just sell all our investments now and hide under our beds. *Before the bubble pops*, while the historic stock market uptrend continues, shouldn't we make some money on it? And if so, is there any way to outperform the market without out-sizing risk?

For decades, most investors attempted to beat the market by picking "good" stocks, meaning stocks that might rise faster than the overall market average. Chapter 5 makes it clear why stock picking has been so appealing and why it no longer works.

Even if beating the market is of no interest to you, simply staying with the old buy-and-hold approach is increasingly risky en route to the Financial Cliff and bubble pop. Clearly, we don't want to hang on too long and watch assets disappear.

So, if stock picking no longer works and buy-and-hold no longer works, what should we do instead? Here's our three-part plan:

1. **Forget Stock Picking.** Instead of individual stocks, choose exchange-traded funds (ETFs) that track the broader stock indexes, such as the S&P 500, Nasdaq 100, and Russell 2000.

2. **Use a Terrific Trading System**. Above all else, you absolutely must have a good trading system that will get you out of the stock market *before* the Financial Cliff. Readers of our earlier *Aftershock* books will remember this is when assets go to Money Heaven. In fact, for those who lack a good trading system, it will feel more like money hell.

Even before the Financial Cliff, there will be plenty of downturns and rebounds. At each stage ahead, having a terrific trading system will allow you to buy low and sell high (or even go short for the short term), while ensuring you avoid the full brunt of the final fall.

3. **Safely Beat the Market – But Only with a Terrific Trading System.** A good trading system can not only save you from the Financial Cliff, it makes it possible to safely beat the market before the Financial Cliff with leveraged market index ETFs. If the mere thought of using leverage instantly alarms you, keep in mind that this option is only safe to pursue with an excellent trading system. Nothing is more important for protection and gains both before and during the Financial Cliff.

The above, in a nutshell, is our game plan for protection AND profit before (including right before) the big Fake Money bubble pop. Now let's look a bit closer at how to execute each of these three steps.

Step 1: Forget Stock Picking, Choose Stock Market Index ETFs

Chapter 5 makes the case that stock picking, while still wildly popular, has proven ineffective for years and is increasingly dangerous in today's investment environment. It is true that you may hit on a temporary winner, but even if you get lucky and buy at just the right time, how will you know when to sell for maximum gains? Most investors won't and don't.

Individual stocks, even the temporary winners, are all subject to potential individual company risks – such as poor management, excessive debt, bad news that hurts the brand, and so on – that can suddenly make the stock drop.

It would be better to skip that kind of avoidable company-related risk and buy the overall market instead. Stock market index ETFs contain a wide mix of individual company stocks, giving you tremendous diversity in a single share.

How much diversity? Well, the ETF representing the S&P 500 index contains 500 companies' stocks, the Nasdaq 100 ETF contains 100 companies, and the Russell 2000 contains, you guessed it, 2000 companies. Individual stock picking is far riskier because it lacks this tremendous diversity.

Even if you pick dozens of individual stocks in order to diversify your portfolio, you are still unlikely to outperform the overall stock market, so why bother? Even one of the best stock pickers of our time, Warren Buffett, has failed and continues to fail to beat the overall stock market. After all the effort involved in detailed expert analysis and careful stock selection, it turns out that simply owning the S&P 500 index ETF (SPY) from June 30, 2013 to June 30, 2021 would have made Buffett a cool 252%. Instead, he made 144%

Clearly, based on decades of evidence, stock market index ETFs are the way to go.

But stock indexes have a big upcoming problem. When the big Fake Money bubble pops – including the stock market bubble – all the stock indexes will tank. And even before the bubble pops, there will be many sudden downturns.

How will you know when to get out of the market to avoid the Financial Cliff? And if you get out of the market prematurely during one of the many coming downturns, how will you know when to get back into the market to take advantage of the temporary rebound?

Fortunately, we have an answer for that.

Step 2: Use a Terrific Trading System

Every investor, whether clinging to stock picking or choosing market index ETFs, is at risk of going over the Financial Cliff. But if you choose the unappealing option of exiting the stock market now, you run the risk of missing out on potential gains before the Financial Cliff.

Regardless of your investment approach, without a good trading system to guide your decisions, you are damned if you do (stay in the market) and damned if you don't.

That means *everyone* in the market needs a good trading system to make money now *and* get out before they lose most of it later.

On the way up, everyone loves a bubble. What could be better or more comfortable than making money in a rising bubble? The discomfort comes when you become *aware* that it's a bubble. You may not know exactly when it will pop but knowing that it's a bubble makes it a lot harder to feel comfortable about any of your investments.

Good! You shouldn't.

If the goal is to make money as long as the bubble keeps rising and also to be ready to exit the stock market before the Financial Cliff, we cannot invest as if the Financial Cliff is not coming. In other words, we *cannot buy and hold.*

Given that the current four-decade-long stock market bubble has lasted for most people's adult lives, if not their entire lives, it's natural for the vast majority of investors to thoroughly believe that, despite occasional declines, the stock market "always comes back." Therefore, you might as well just sit back and stay put (buy and hold). Adding a little "rebalancing" of one's portfolio mix each year creates the illusion of staying on top of it.

But in fact, the vast majority of investors are not staying on top of it. In a rising bubble, most investors are simply being swept along as the bubble goes up, and they will continue to be swept along when the stock market bubble pops and plunges over the Financial Cliff.

In a bubble, most buy-and-hold investors reliably make money on the way up, and then, just as reliably, they will lose money – in this case, *a lot of money* – on the way down. The higher the bubble goes, the steeper the bubble drops later.

The big problem facing every stock market investor is the fact that all current gains are actually Fake Money, meaning it won't last. **If you want to be able to keep this money, you absolutely have to sell all your stock positions before the Financial Cliff**. Otherwise, not only will you lose your gains, but you will also lose most of the principal you invested to get those gains.

So, getting out before the market goes over the Cliff is essential. The challenge, however, is that that not every little downturn or even every big downturn is the beginning of the Financial Cliff.

In the recent past, the market has shown a tendency to bounce back fairly quickly – most notably in March 2020. But whether you get back in quickly or a bit more slowly, the key is that you do get back in. *Until we hit the Financial Cliff, we are still in a bull market.*

The Financial Cliff is a one-time event. Hence, you cannot let yourself be scared out of the market, like a scared rabbit, every time the market takes a downturn. In the stock market there are bulls and bears, but no rabbits. Rabbits just get run over. Instead of fear, you need a very good trading system that can keep you in the market making money and get you out of the market before those gains (and your principal) evaporate.

Fortunately, we have something for that.

Introducing an Exceptional Trading System That Can Beat the Market Now and Avoid the Financial Cliff Later

Instead of a dangerous buy-and-hold strategy that is destined to end very poorly, the ideal trading system will help us "buy low and sell high" – and also decisively get out of the market before the everything goes seriously south.

To achieve these goals, we need a trading system that can . . .

1. **Accurately identify new market trends** – this is essential for avoiding the Financial Cliff, and for distinguishing between big swings and big downtrends before the Financial Cliff.
2. **Reduce risk** through diversification and correct trend identification.
3. **Provide protection from the big Fake Money bubble pop**, without knowing *when* it will pop.
4. **Beat the market before it pops.**

Accurately Identifying New Market Trends Is Key

Taking advantage of market ups and downs would be relatively easy if the market would cooperate by simply rising and falling smoothly over a long period of time. In a smooth long-term trend, you can simply buy long positions in a clear uptrend and buy short positions in a clear downtrend.

But, alas, the market is not so cooperative. Longer-term up markets often contain down periods, and longer-term down markets often contain up periods. Sometimes these fluctuations are quite large (without being a new trend), and sometimes these seemingly random movements may continue without any clear overall trend for a long time.

Without the benefit of 20/20 hindsight, how do you know if any given fluctuation is the beginning of the next up or down trend, instead of being a short-term reversal within a longer-term trend? Or maybe it's just a period of higher volatility within a period of no long-term trend at all?

To make money (aka, buy low and sell high), you have to accurately identify new trends AND enter long and short positions early (buy low) without going in too early or too late. If you buy too soon, there's a chance that no new trend will materialize. If you buy too late (because you were waiting for the trend to become more obvious), there's a chance you will miss your opportunity to get in early enough to make a profit.

In order to buy low and sell high, we have to find the sweet spot. Like Goldilocks: not too early and not too late.

To find this sweet spot, many stock analysts over the years have tried to create mathematical models to estimate the probability of the future. In other words, they tried to determine the odds that any given trade will be profitable in the future based on how the price of a given asset moved in the past.

Not surprisingly, the purely mathematical approach to investing does not work too well because stock market movements are not entirely rational and changing investor psychology is highly unpredictable at any given time. Some of these mathematically based trading systems seem to work well some of the time. But that's because just about every trading system seems to work some of the time, especially in a relentlessly rising bubble.

Unfortunately, the opposite is also true: **just about every trading system fails to work in a dramatically falling bubble, the timing of which no one can accurately predict.**

The key to a profitable and protective trading system is the ability to accurately identify and take advantage of newly forming trends. We do not need to know ahead of time how long any given trend will last or if it will later become the big bubble pop.

What we need is a trading system that is very good at catching the beginning of new market trends – both up and down – *not too early that we get faked out, and not too late that we get left out.*

Such a trading system is not hypothetical. The authors of this book spent years developing, and have recently deployed, such a trading system. While no trading system can predict the future or deliver 100% accuracy, our active trading system is able to correctly identify and take advantage of newly forming up and down trends. Obviously, we cannot reveal details of our "secret sauce," but it's important to understand how our proprietary trading system achieves the goals listed above.

The first, and by far the most important, is the ability to *successfully identify and catch new market trends.* Our proprietary trading system uses a combination of mathematical modeling, advanced charting techniques, and other key elements to identify new up and down trends.

A new "trend" means a market movement is a generally up or generally down direction over the course of at least two weeks. But it is also important that we do not wait too long to enter a new up or down trend. Our trading system does not chase market trends, which guarantees losses. Identifying and entering new trends correctly is key.

Reduce Risk with Diversification and Accurate Trend Identification

As mentioned earlier, the use of market index ETFs provides risk protection through enormous diversification.

However, no amount of diversification of stocks will help you when the highly correlated and overvalued stock market plunges over the Financial Cliff. That's where accurate trend identification becomes the ultimate form of risk management, far better than mere diversification alone can ever be

A big advantage of a trading system that correctly identifies both up and down stock market trends is that it is inherently risk averse. For example, if a stock market index changes from an uptrend to a downtrend, we don't simply hold onto the index in the belief that the uptrend will re-appear at some point. We sell the index and have the option of buying shorts (actually inverse ETFs) on the index, if our system determines it is the start of a significant downtrend. We don't hold a position "into the wind" on the basis of market conviction or detailed analysis telling us the winds will soon change.

While we have a strong conviction of where the market will go in the longer term, we have no conviction on where the market will go in the shorter term. Although conviction is often crucial to most money managers who are picking undervalued stocks or other assets, our trading system requires no conviction, and that substantially lowers our risk.

Our macro view is still fully intact, but on a day-to-day basis it is our trading system that makes the call to buy, sell, or hold. Accurate trend identification is key. While no system is correct all the time, being correct more often than incorrect is essential.

Accurately identifying a change in the market trend helps limit risk in two ways. First, actively moving from the long side to the short side of an investment position (or to cash) when the market trend changes, greatly helps minimize losses. Stock indices are not held long or short for a long time if the market is moving in the opposite direction. If the market is experiencing short-term volatility, the system will move out of the market entirely, but those times are rare.

Second, by making good gains in significant up and down trends, any smaller losses during small trends are offset. Risk is reduced by making more gains than losses when holding longs or shorts.

By the way, our trading system does not require buying shorts in order to make good gains and limit risk. Furthermore, if we do choose a short position, we *do not use direct shorts*, only long ETFs that short the underlying asset. That means we use inverse ETFs to take a short position. These ETFs go up when the underlying stock index ETF goes down. This is much safer than shorting an index due to the risks and costs involved in actually borrowing stock to short. Inverse ETFs can be expensive to hold long term but, generally, we hold inverse ETFs for far less time than non-inverse ETFs. The opportunities to short are almost always very short.

Protection and Profits When the Bubble Pops

Every investor, whether they currently know it or not, is in trouble. And there is only one guaranteed way to avoid this trouble: **do not be in the stock market when it hits the Financial Cliff!**

You can get out and stay out now, but you will very likely miss out on some big gains to come. Or you can get in and stay in, and plunge over the Cliff with just about everyone else.

Or you can follow our profit and protection plan with the trading system described above.

But whatever you do, you cannot know now what will happen later or when it will happen. When future stock market downturns occur, you will not know which one of these big drops is the start of the Financial Cliff. No one knows the future.

The advantage of our trading system is you don't have to identify which downturn will turn out to be THE Big One. The system will move out of market longs and perhaps into market shorts, whether it is the bubble pop or not.

In fact, when the Big One finally hits, the system will see it as just another profitable downtrend and be out of the market and shorting it long before any of us know it's the Big One.

Once you are out of the market, the opportunities to make money don't come to a screeching halt. Instead, new opportunities will open up. These include investing in precious metals, investing in income-producing distressed assets, as well as other opportunities that will arise after the Financial Cliff.

As we get near the Financial Cliff, we will discuss the opportunities available in much more detail. But, it's worth knowing that good investment opportunities don't cease when the market falls off the Financial Cliff. In fact, some of the best investment opportunities in history will open up after the Financial Cliff. Having some money to invest will be a huge advantage at that point.

Other Great Benefits

Making money now and avoiding the Financial Cliff later are not the only important advantages of a great trading system.

For those who want to pursue even greater gains before the Financial Cliff, our protection and profit plan has one more innovative step you may want to consider . . .

Step 3: Reliably Beat the Market – But Only with a Great Trading System

By now we hope we have convinced you to give up stock picking and rely on stock market index ETFs instead, with the help of a great trading system.

But alas, there is one big problem with owning an ETF that tracks a stock market index: **you can never beat the stock market with a market index ETF because the market index is the stock market!**

There is a simple way around this barrier: *use levered stock index ETFs.* But you can only do so safely if you have a very good trading system. Without a good reliable trading system, all investing will eventually cost you dearly, and if you use leverage without a good trading system, it will cost you even more dearly.

Having a great trading system is essential, but using leverage is not. You can easily skip this step of our protection and profits plan by choosing stock index ETFs and deploying a good trading system, without using levered stock index ETFs. That's all you need to make gains in the market now and get out of the market before the bubble pops later.

However, if you want to beat the market with at least some portion of your investments, our goal here is to show you enough charts and address enough questions about using levered stock index ETFs so that you can at least consider this approach.

Why Use Levered Stock Index ETFs?

Because it's the best way to reliably beat the market.

If you buy the ETF for the stock index S&P 500, for example, "SPY," you are buying an asset that tracks the ups and downs of the S&P. Many investors use the S&P 500 as the normal benchmark for "the market." So, by definition, if you buy SPY, you'll never beat the market. But, of course, you will never lag the market either.

In the past, one way many investors outperformed the S&P 500 was to invest in the NASDAQ 100 ETF ("QQQ"). The NASDAQ 100 is composed primarily of technology stocks and therefore tends to outperform the broader-based S&P 500, which is composed of a wide range of stocks that underperform the tech stocks over the long term.

Tech stocks tend to lead the market when it is going up, but they also lead the market when it is going down. So, they are generally bad in a bear market and good in a bull market. Hence, as long as the market is generally going up, technology stocks have been a pretty good bet for beating the S&P.

A riskier way to beat the market has been to use sector ETFs. These are ETFs that hold a basket of stocks in a particular sector, like homebuilding (XHB) or defense stocks (ITA). These sectors can often outperform the market because that industry or sector may be doing better than the market for industry-specific reasons, such as a home-buying frenzy, or increased government spending on, say, the military. Some sectors might do better because they were previously doing much worse in an economic downturn. For example, airlines (JETS) got hit hard in the Covid recession and then came back strongly at the end of 2020.

With industry-sector ETFs, there are often multiple ETFs available. Generally, all of these sectors or stock index ETFs have low fees because they are not managed ETFs. They have no fund managers that must be paid. The ETF simply holds a basket of stocks. Not every ETF has low fees and no manager, however, so it's worth checking into that before buying one. With this type of investing, you should always favor low-fee, non-managed ETFs.

But none of these approaches comes close to the benefits of using levered stock index ETFs.

The Power of Levered Stock Index ETFs

You can easily and reliably beat the market (the S&P) with a double-levered S&P ETF. How much will you beat the market with a double-levered S&P ETF? Twice as much! Or, even better, you can triple your gains with a triple-levered S&P 500 index ETF. As long as the market goes up, you will always beat the market with a levered S&P ETF.

Maybe you consider a double- or triple-levered ETF of the S&P 500 too risky. But why is it any riskier than buying an ETF of the S&P that is not levered *if your strategy is to buy and hold?* The movements of a levered S&P ETF closely track the S&P 500. If you would own the S&P, why not own double or triple the S&P?

Plus, these ETFs are extremely liquid – SSO, the double levered S&P 500 ETF trades almost 2 million shares per day. If you want to sell it, you easily can.

Levered stock market index ETFs make lots of money in a rising stock market. Need some proof? Let's take a look at the performance of double- and triple-levered ETFs on the S&P 500 in the last 10 years shown in Figures 6.1, 6.2, and 6.3.

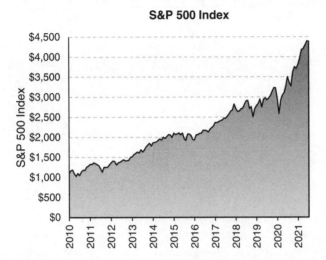

Figure 6.1   Notice Any Difference in These Three Price Charts from February 26, 2010 to August 2, 2021?

Source: Standard & Poor's.

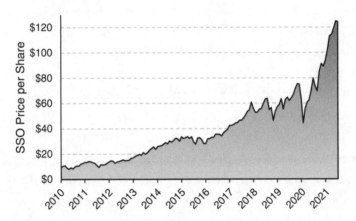

Figure 6.2   S&P 500 Index Double-Levered ETF (SSO)

Source: Standard & Poor's.

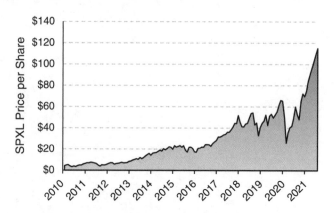

Figure 6.3   S&P 500 Index Triple-Levered ETF (SPXL)
Source: Standard & Poor's.

Not Much Difference in These Charts . . . Except Performance

All three charts above look more or less the same, with similar changes in direction, up and down. But two of these charts *way outperformed* the S&P during the last 10 years.

The first chart, the S&P 500, went up about 297%.

The second chart, SSO, a double-levered S&P 500 ETF, went up about 1226%.

The third chart, SPXL, a triple-levered S&P 500 ETF, went up about 2606%.

There is little difference in their movements. They all follow each other nearly perfectly. The levered S&P 500 ETFs go down a lot more, but they also go up a lot more. Most importantly, their up-and-down movements are completely in tandem with the S&P 500.

This is the kind of market outperformance that many active fund managers would die for.

More Advantages of Levered ETFs

Beyond great performance, levered stock index ETFs have other advantages, too.

Sometimes investors use leverage by buying a stock on margin. Not only does this create a debt that must eventually be repaid, it also creates margin call risk – that is, the risk that the stock value drops, you get a margin call, can't pay it, and are forced to sell your stock at a fire sale price, only to later see the stock price bounce right back up.

However, when you own a levered stock index ETF, there is no margin call risk. No debt is incurred; therefore you won't have to answer any margin calls.

Also, just like nonlevered stock index ETFs, levered stock index ETFs have all the inherent advantages of any stock index ETF, including very high diversification and relatively limited volatility.

And because market index ETF movements almost exactly track a major highly diversified index, such as the S&P 500, there is no need to hunt for a great set of risky high-performing stocks and then have to hold them during big price decreases that are way out of line with the market.

These ETFs, both levered and nonlevered, always move with the market; so there are no unusual moves to put fear into your heart that you have bet on the wrong stock. If you believe in the stock market long term, levered stock index ETFs on the highly diversified market index S&P 500 are the best way to make far more money than the stock market. A double-levered index ETF or triple-levered index ETF is the simplest and easiest way to beat the market by a huge margin. You get almost the exact same movement as the overall market, just way bigger and without the threat of margin calls.

Want to beat a levered S&P ETF? Try a levered Nasdaq ETF.

Over the long term, NASDAQ has historically outperformed the S&P 500. That's because it contains more high-growth stocks. Even though it has only 100 stocks, rather than

500 like the S&P 500, it is still highly diversified. It has sharper short-term ups and downs, but over the long term, it way outperforms the S&P. In fact, since January 2, 1980, the NASDAQ Composite Index is up 9,808%, whereas the S&P 500 is only up 3817%, as of August 2, 2021.

Let's look at the performance of NASDAQ 100 levered ETFs over last 10 years, just as we did with the S&P 500.

From February 26, 2010, to August 2, 2021, the NASDAQ 100 was up about 724%. Not bad, and much better than the S&P 500.

However, a double-levered Nasdaq 100 ETF, QLV, was up about 4194%.

But, even more impressive, a triple-levered NASDAQ 100 ETF, TQQQ, was up 12,049% in that period as shown in Figure 6.4. Wow, is all you can say!

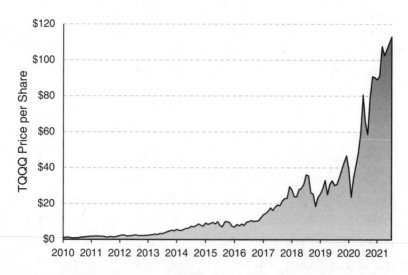

Figure 6.4   TQQQ (triple-levered NASDAQ 100 ETF) from February 26, 2010, to August 2, 2021

Source: NASDAQ.

February 2, 2010, to August 2, 2021, the NASDAQ 100 was up 297%. However, TQQQ was up 12,049%. Wow!

Warren Buffett's Stock Picking Folly—Here's a Much Better All-In Bet on America

If Warren Buffett had just put his money into this one highly diversified investment in 500 large-cap stocks (a double- or triple-levered S&P 500 ETF), he would have performed far better and handily beaten the market in the last 10 years as shown in Figure 6.5.

Figure 6.5   Rate of Return for Berkshire Hathaway (Warren Buffett) and SPXL (triple-levered S&P 500) June 30, 2013 to August 2, 2021

This would have been a much better all-in bet on American business than Buffett's highly concentrated investments in banking stocks, insurance stocks, and his big bets on Kraft Heinz and Burlington Northern railroad (which he called an all-in bet on America). But, of course, it wouldn't be a stock picker's bet. It would just be a great investment.

Four Big Concerns About Levered Stock Index ETFs

The first concern we have already discussed – leverage is dangerous. As we pointed out, levered stock index ETFs are far less dangerous than buying on margin because you are not incurring a debt and will not get a margin call.

Additionally, there are a lot of levered ETFs out there, and many are quite volatile, and some have even gone out of business. This is true. You need to be careful when using levered ETFs.

That's why we only talk about using levered stock index ETFs. Levered stock index ETFs are inherently much less volatile than an industry ETF that is levered. Or an investment-strategy ETF that is levered.

That's because of the inherent stability of a major stock index, such as the S&P 500. It makes a stock index levered ETF far less vulnerable to wild swings. And, they are very liquid, unlike like some levered ETFs.

A second concern many investors have is that levered ETFs are not for long-term investing. This is true. Many levered ETFs are just trading tools. They are meant for short-term trading and hedging.

However, when you look at the long-term performance of levered stock index ETFs, as we just did, you can see that the long-term performance is quite good and the movements very much follow the market's movements.

The third concern many investors have about levered ETFs is that they are very volatile. This is true. And, again, this is why we only discuss using levered **stock index ETFs**, such as for the S&P 500. As a major stock index, it is inherently less volatile than industry ETFs, or strategy ETFs or small market index ETFs. However, since it is levered, it is more volatile than the S&P 500. Hence, this is why we stress it is important to have a good trading system even when using a major stock index levered ETF.

The fourth concern is that levered stock index ETFs lose money over time due to "leakage" from daily rebalancing. This is true. However, as you can see, the long-term, and even the short-term performance of a major stock index levered ETF, does not show a great deal of leakage that isn't more than offset by higher performance.

Inverse levered ETFs are very different. These are ETFs that short stocks. Their leakage rate tends to be greater than the rate of regular ETFs. More importantly, they generally don't work for long periods of time because the opportunity to short a market tends to be very short.

Remember, from an overall stock investing standpoint, your biggest risk protection, by far, comes from having a great trading system that can accurately identify market trends. Without the proper trading system, every investment – levered or not – is an enormous risk.

The Real Risk of Levered Stock Index ETFs

The elephant in the room, of course, is that any ETF that goes up at double or triple the stock market will also go down at that same double or triple rate. That means you can lose a lot more money with a levered stock index ETF when the stock market declines than you would with a non-levered index ETF. And with compounding, the losses will grow even bigger over time in a long-term bear market.

The problem is, even when it is not a long-term bear market, you may get scared out of your position and sell during a big temporary drop. Of course, selling due to fear is also a problem for investors in a non-levered index ETF or any investment, but the addition of leverage makes it a lot easier to get a lot more scared because each drop is magnified due to leverage.

That is why *you must have an excellent trading system* to use leverage. Without an effective trading system, a 10% drop on the S&P means a 30% or more loss on SPXL (a 3× levered S&P ETF). Without a great trading system, the use of leverage may scare you into selling sooner and more often during temporary declines. If you sell out of your position and the market then goes back up, you could get stuck with locking-in realized losses that you could have avoided. This is true for all investments, but more so for levered ETFs.

Increased fear when using levered ETFs is a significant risk factor that can lead to poor performance over time as markets do occasionally decline temporarily. The best way to deal with this understandable fear is to use an excellent trading system.

Of course, without a great trading system, you are in trouble once you hit the Financial Cliff, even if you never use leverage.

Why Most Investors Won't Even Consider Leveraged Stock Index ETFs

No money manager, including Warren Buffett, would ever suggest putting your money into a double- or triple-levered S&P 500 ETF, even though it is as safe as any diversified portfolio of stocks and clearly has much higher returns.

Why is that?

Well, for starters, if everyone invested in stock market index ETFs, whether levered or nonlevered, what would be the use of a money manager or a great stock picker like Buffett? Stock salespeople would never recommend it. How would they sell you any stocks with this strategy? And levered ETFs kill any reason to try to beat the market with stock picking. Without stock picking, there would be no stock-picking jobs. Wall Street certainly doesn't want that.

But there is a more fundamental reason why they don't like market index ETFs. Investors who only invest in index funds or similar ETFs do not help push the market back up after big downturns. For stock salespeople and money managers, keeping their careers alive fully depends on pushing up the market after every downturn.

If everyone invested in stock indices – whether non-levered, double-levered, or triple-levered – the stock market bubble would pop. By avoiding these types of investments, money managers are hurting their performance incredibly. But they are more than willing to sacrifice performance in order to do their part to help keep the stock bubble alive, which is critical to their long-term success and critical to the continuance of the overall Fake Money bubble economy.

If any of these people really believed that the US stock market was a good long-term investment, then they should also believe that the S&P 500 is a good investment, right? And, if they really believed in the S&P 500, there's no better place to be than a double- or triple-levered S&P 500 ETF.

If stock market believers aren't willing to buy double or triple the market index, we have to wonder if they really are all that sold on stocks, or are they just cheering the markets onward and upward because they know the alternative is a massive collapse of the big Fake Money bubble economy.

Beyond Stocks, Other Ways to Protect and Grow Wealth Before It's Too Late

If actively trading the stock market with a unique trading system is not for you, there are other options for protection and potential growth as we move closer to the Financial Cliff.

1. Buy gold and close your eyes.
2. Get a low fixed-rate home mortgage while you still can.
3. Go to cash and give up income and capital gains.

Gold

The best buy-and-hold investment for the last 20 years will be the best buy-and-hold investment for at least the next 10 years.

For thousands of years, most of the world has considered gold as a reliable store of value. True, there have been periods in the past when the price of gold traveled a rocky road. For example, while the stock market was rapidly rising from 1980 to 2000, gold did not perform well.

But for the last two decades, gold has far and away outperformed stocks. Gold is up 560%, whereas the S&P 500, even with dividends reinvested, (S&P 500 TR), is only up about 380% (as of July 1, 2021) as you can see in Figure 6.6.

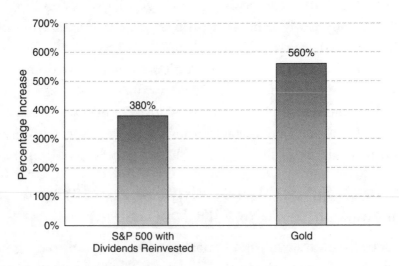

Figure 6.6   The Performance of Gold vs. the S&P 500 from January 2, 2000 to July 1, 2021

Unlike in many other countries, investing in gold in the United States can be socially awkward. American investors seem to instinctively dislike gold, maybe because we tend to see buying gold as the equivalent to betting against the home team. It may feel unpatriotic to bet against the future success of the stock market and other US assets.

Not only that, to some people, buying gold may make you seem like a "prepper," someone who expects the sky to fall and therefore has an underground bunker and two years' worth of food.

But gold is not just for preppers. In fact, you don't even need to believe the bubble will ever pop. Think of buying gold as a kind of insurance policy – just in case. The greater your concern, the more you should own.

Also, gold won't go down when interest rates rise, unlike stocks, bonds, and real estate.

Going forward, gold may not rise in a straight line. (In fact, the price is just about guaranteed to drop the day after you buy it!) But gold will do very well in the lead-up to and after the stock market bubble pop.

That's because, despite most Americans disliking gold, the US is less than 5% of the world's population. In most other countries, many people think of gold as a good store of value, feel comfortable buying gold, and will rush into gold and drive up its price as the global bubble pops in just about every economy.

So you can continue to dislike gold if you wish, just make sure you own some! Preferably at least some of it as physical gold, such as gold coins or bars.

Get a Low Fixed-Rate Mortgage While You Still Can

Another potential way to make money outside of the stock market is with real estate.

However, there is a very big caveat to this advice that you must not ignore: Real estate values will dramatically fall in the Financial Cliff when interest rates rise dramatically, and may also decline to some extent before that, as well. As values drop, real estate will become increasingly illiquid, meaning it will become harder and harder to sell quickly, or at all.

Before that occurs, real estate can be a potential money maker, especially if you can find a bargain and flip for a profit to an able buyer without holding it for too long.

What about a place to live? Many people have been asking us: *Should I buy a home while prices are roaring during the pandemic?*

A lot depends on your personal circumstances, but in general, given how high home prices have risen during the pandemic, the question is should you buy now or wait for prices to go down?

To answer that, let's look at why home prices are up: (1) a buying frenzy caused by the Covid pandemic and (2) record low mortgage rates, with fixed-rate 30-year mortgages close to or under 3%.

Will the Covid-based buying frenzy continue for much longer? Probably not. There's no particular reason it will end other than the fact that frenzies tend to be short term because they quickly clear out the people most interested in buying a home.

More important than the fading frenzy, the key to house prices continuing to go up is interest rates. In a normal economy, rising inflation, as we are seeing now, should push interest rates higher. But this is no normal economy. Instead, it is an economy that is highly dependent on maintaining ultra-low interest rates. In particular, the stock market and real estate markets are highly dependent on interest rates staying very low. Rising interest rates would be a huge negative for both stocks and real estate.

So, the normal pressures that push the Federal Reserve to raise interest rates are offset by the critical need to keep interest rates low, even as inflation moves higher. At some point, the Fed may attempt to raise interest rates, but it will quickly find that doing so (or even implying that it might do so) creates big problems with the stock and real estate markets. If the recent past is any guide, the Fed reacts quickly to such problems by keeping rates the same or pushing them even lower.

That means mortgage rates are likely to stay low, which will help maintain current or higher home prices. The frenzy will fade, and home prices likely won't rise as fast as they did in 2020, but due to continued very low interest rates, home prices are not likely to fall much either.

If you want or need to buy a home, the best way to play this situation of high prices that likely won't come down much in the near future is to get a *fixed-rate mortgage* and minimize your down payment. If prices continue to rise, great.

However, if and when (and we definitely think it is only a matter of when), interest rates rise, the fact that you have a *low interest fixed-rate mortgage* will shove the risk of rising interest rates onto the bank. That really means you are shifting the risk to the government, given that they guarantee most of the mortgages made in this country.

With your monthly payment fixed and your income rising with inflation to some extent, it actually becomes *cheaper and cheaper* to make your mortgage payment. In fact, if we get high lasting inflation, which we eventually expect, that monthly fixed rate mortgage payment will become cheaper and cheaper to make year after year.

With that in mind, it's also worth remembering that taking on a lot of debt to buy a house you can't really afford is always a risk if you have to sell quickly. Prices can fall after you buy a house and you will take a loss. Or, if your income is unstable, you are taking a risk that you can't make the mortgage payments. These are always the risks in any housing market. They are simply heightened in a high-priced market.

The bottom line is that if you are waiting for a big short-term fall, don't count on it. However, if you are waiting for the current frenzy to cool a bit, that's possible, but again, there is something of a floor on current home prices due to low interest rates that are not likely to change much in the near future.

Finally, all real estate is local, so while national issues like interest rates are important, they are by no means the only factor in determining prices.

Cash

The easiest (and in the short term, the safest) strategy is simply to get out of the stock market and go to cash. If you have been in the market for a while, you have had a good run. Instead of pushing your luck by staying in much longer, you can take your gains now, or soon, and get out.

Stashing cash will not hurt you in the short term. Money markets and CDs pay near zero interest these days, but at least you won't have to worry about future stock market volatility and the coming multiple downtrends ahead, culminating in a huge plunge over the Financial Cliff. Sitting that out has its anti-stress benefits.

However, what you will have to worry about in the longer term is **inflation** (see Chapter 3). Even just 5–10% inflation will eat away at the buying power of your cash, increasingly evaporating your wealth as inflation continues to rise.

So, while cashing out of your vulnerable investments is fine in the short term, it will not help you in the longer term. The inevitable inflation ahead means Cash will not be King forever.

Fake Money . . . Real Support

There is real danger ahead, and we all need to prepare for what will likely be a devastating blow to investments, livelihoods, and wealth.

For the latest updates as we approach the inevitable Financial Cliff and Aftershock ahead, please visit www .fakemoneyrealdanger.com or www.aftershockpublishing .com.

There you can also sign up to receive any of our email alert services – *all 100% free.*

Or contact us at 703-787-0139 or info@aftershock publishing.com.

For private consulting for individuals, businesses, and groups, please contact *Fake Money, Real Danger* and *Aftershock* coauthor Cindy Spitzer at 443-980-7367 or information@ arksma.com Your first call is free.

For hands-on investment management based on the macroeconomic views and investment strategies described in our books, please contact Ark Financial Management at 703-774-3520, 888-238-8370 or information@arksma.com.

CHAPTER 7

How the Big Fake Money
Bubble Will Pop

Although we can't predict exactly when the big Fake Money bubble will pop, we now have much more information to help estimate how and when it might happen.

For example, we now know more about how the economy and markets react to massive money printing and how reluctant businesses have been to raise prices.

We also know more about how much the government is likely to borrow and print over the next few years. In the summer of 2018, the Fed wasn't printing money at all. At that time, we didn't know when they would print again or how much. Now, in 2021, we have a much better idea of both.

That allows us to create the framework of a potential timeline. While no exact dates are predictable, we can now make a good estimate about the stages of the timeline and roughly when they may occur.

Knowing the Timing the Bubble Pop Is Important – But Only to Stock Pickers

Although we can make a good estimate of the stages of the bubble pop, the exact timing is impossible to know. However, *from an investment standpoint, there is no need to know the exact timing.* The reason so many people would like to know the exact timing is because they are trying to do stock picking. Being able to pick the proper buy and sell points on a stock is an essential part of good stock picking. Hence, knowing the timing of when stocks will go down, or up, is very important.

Since we have already pointed out how difficult (next to impossible) stock picking is for the best stock pickers in the world in Chapter 5, you really shouldn't be very focused on trying to time the bubble pop.

What you should be focused on is finding an excellent trading system that will help you through what will likely be a complex "popping sequence," regardless of exactly when it starts.

With an excellent trading system, trying to "time" the pop is pointless. However, from a non-investment timing standpoint, how the Fake Money bubble will go through the stages that lead to the final pop is absolutely fascinating.

With Massive Stimulus, the Post-Covid Bull Market Will Continue

Massive stimulus from both Congress and the Fed will keep pushing the market up. If they don't provide enough stimulus, the market will go down. If it doesn't come back up fairly quickly, it will go down further. Going down quickly will send a message to Congress and the Fed that they need to do more stimulus. And they will do whatever it takes.

In addition, the stock market knows up is good and down is bad. More than that, they know it's a bubble market and is vulnerable to popping. Hence, they will try hard to keep the market up. They may not even need a big increase in stimulus to keep it up. They are already getting massive amounts.

But if they do need more, it'll be there. We are simply too far down the Fake Money bubble road to change direction now. We must keep the markets up or they will collapse. Because these are bubbles, there is no in-between alternative.

At this point, we either do what it takes to support the bubbles, or we fail to keep them going and the bubbles pop.

Not that there won't be corrections or maybe even a rare bear market, but for the most part, the Covid stock market boom should be followed by a post–Covid boom bull market. It certainly won't go up as fast as it did in the year after the March Covid collapse, and there will likely be a lot of concern over it being a bubble market, but despite all the worries, it is likely to still go up.

If it doesn't, Congress and the Fed will make sure it does.

The Bull Market Ends with an Inflation Awakening

This is where it starts to get interesting. At some point, the markets will fear, not cheer, more money printing. That's a direct quote from our earlier *Aftershock* books, and it is still quite accurate. In particular, the Fed will print more money to keep interest rates low (nothing new there), but this time, instead of pushing the stock market up further, Wall Street will see that this money printing is creating more inflation.

That's when investors start to fear money printing. That fear, of course, only grows worse when investors also see interest rates climb, despite the Fed printing more money to buy bonds. Interest rates are rising because private investors want interest rates that better compensate them for rising inflation. The Fed cannot stop that.

So, Wall Street will begin to see that the Fed is between a rock and a hard place. It can't keep printing money to keep rates low without causing more inflation. And, even if it prints a lot of money to buy bonds, interest rates are rising.

Hence, it is easy to see that the Fed will need to print even more money to keep rates from rising too fast, which will create even more inflation and, thus, some on Wall Street can see this is not going to end well.

They were hoping (actually counting on) that massive money printing *would not* cause significant long-lasting inflation. Or, alternatively, they were counting on the Fed being able to easily reduce money printing without increasing interest rates significantly.

At that point, however, it will be proven to some on Wall Street that neither dream will come true.

This inflation awakening could take a while, though. For one thing, inflation could easily fall temporarily. No question that some of the inflation we are seeing in 2021 is simply due to constrained supply and a big jump in demand. This is *transitory* inflation, as the Fed likes to say. It's not real inflation. It's just supply and demand pricing doing what it should do. Once supply and demand come into balance, prices will stop rising as fast.

In addition, the inflation awakening could take a while because Wall Street may feel that the Fed can fight inflation by letting interest rates rise a bit. However, any significant increase in rates will have a big negative effect on this very-high-priced stock market. Hence, the Fed will be forced to back off of any more increases and will probably decrease rates.

Again, a temporary decrease in inflation and an attempt by the Fed to let rates rise only postpones Wall Street's inflation awakening. It does not solve the underlying problem.

This is when it gets really interesting. Why? Because it's so unpredictable. The market will be increasingly faced with what is so incredibly obvious that some in the market will actually point it out: The Fed cannot control inflation without raising interest rates a lot – more like what Paul Volcker did in the early 1980s.

And investors quietly know this bubble stock market can't handle the truth of high interest rates, as it did in the 1980s. Back then, the Dow was at 1000. Today it's at 35,000. This market can only exist with low interest rates. High interest rates will simply collapse the market.

Again, getting to the inflation awakening will take a while because the market will need solid evidence, as outlined above, before a small group can reach this conclusion.

This is where the market starts to flatten out (Figure 7.1). Decreases in the market can be offset by stock market animal spirits and Fed/congressional stimulus, but it will be hard to keep hitting higher highs. It is the end of the post-Covid bull market.

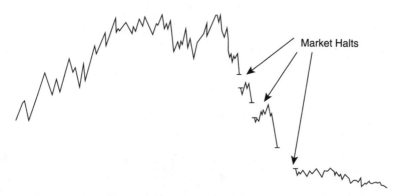

Figure 7.1 A Likely Future for the Stock Market

The likely future for the stock market includes a continuation of the post-Covid bull market followed by an inflation awakening that ends the bull market. After what is likely a short period of increasing volatility with little net up or down movement, the market will enter into a series of downward cycles with lower highs and lower lows. The cycles will be punctuated by times when the stock market is halted in an effort to keep the market from falling further. This will end with a final downward plunge that will be the Financial Cliff.

As the Bull Market Ends, the Fake Money Bear Awakens and Multiple Down Cycles Begin

The end of the post Covid bull market will likely trigger a short period of increasing volatility but little net up or down movement. After this relatively flat yet volatile period, the market will enter into a series of downward trending cycles with lower highs and lower lows.

At first these will be modest downward cycles. But, over time, the cycles will become larger and larger. During the later stages of these downward cycles, there could be several attempts to stop the collapse by closing the markets. Brief market pauses combined with desperate animal spirits could cause some massive rallies.

But, ultimately, they will be ineffective because the fundamental problem of the Fed being forced to print massive amounts of money, which creates more and more inflation, cannot be solved without first creating very high interest rates that collapse the stock, bond, and real estate markets.

The Last Down Cycle Triggers the Financial Cliff

When Wall Street sees that brief market closures cannot solve the problem of the Fed's financial medicine of massive money printing becoming the poison of massive inflation, there will be an inevitable panic that collapses the market.

It's not at all clear how many downward cycles it will take to reach the final downward cycle of the Financial Cliff. More than two and less than seven is a broad guess. Nor do we know how deep the plunges and how big the rebounds will be, prior to the final Financial Cliff.

This is where a good trading system is absolutely essential.

What we do know is that it will end in a panic causing the Financial Cliff.

Once the Market Goes Down Over the Financial Cliff, It Won't Come Back Up for a Long, Long Time

A stock picker might think that after the Financial Cliff is a perfect time to pick up some very low-priced stocks that can be flipped for a nice profit in a few years, or even a few months. Unfortunately, at this point, the economy and stock market will be undergoing a fundamental transformation.

The economy can only recover through increases in productivity, which are very hard, will be intensely fought, and are very slow to improve the economy.

Without a growing economy to grow the stock market, and without the conditions that allowed the stock market bubble to outpace the economy, the stock market cannot and will not ever be a source of big easy profits again.

Instead, the market will eventually revert to its primary function – a secondary market that buys stocks from primary investors who want liquidity. There is some profit in providing liquidity, but not much.

The only significant profits are made in real investments that are primary investments – investments where the money is invested directly into the company to help increase its revenues and profits.

The key to making a profit on those investments will be buying assets that can be used to make a profit. That means buying the assets cheap and managing those assets very well to make a profit. For a while after the Financial Cliff, this will become extremely profitable because capital is scarce, and the risks and performance demands are high.

Investors will only invest if the profits are very high. That means that asset values will be pushed very low. Stock and real estate values in particular will be pushed low by investors looking to make big profits with those assets.

But even hard assets, such as machinery, will be priced low for the same reason. Eventually, as machinery is used up and scrapped, prices for the remaining used machinery will rise. But likely at that point a lot of machinery will have lost most of its useful life. Once there is little used machinery available, it will have to be priced at what it costs to make it.

So, after the Financial Cliff the investing environment will be extremely profitable, but not for stock pickers. Instead, it will be profitable for people who invest in the assets of bankrupted companies and manage them well to make a big profit. There will be opportunities for this that are both big and small. Some service business will actually require very little capital to create and can make big profits.

Bottom line – the only source of significant wealth after the Financial Cliff will be profits, not higher valuation of assets. To make high profits, asset prices will be pushed low by investors and will have to stay low. No rebound. It's all hard money at that point, just as all economic growth is hard growth.

Economic growth will not come from the financial wizardry of massive government borrowing that can't be paid off and massive money printing to support it. Instead, it will have to come from *productivity growth*, especially in the big service sectors of education, healthcare, government services, financial services, real estate, transportation, and utilities.

It's hard work and it's not a ton of fun, but it's real. And, in the end, **REAL money beats Fake Money every time**.

CHAPTER 8

What If We're Wrong? Great, You'll Make Tons of Money in the Ever-Rising Stock Market!

What if we are wrong and all this money we are massively printing and borrowing is not Fake Money but actually real money?

In a sense, as long as it doesn't create inflation, it IS real money! As long as it doesn't cause inflation, your stock investments will continue to make more and more money in a continually rising stock market driven higher and higher by more and more massive money printing and borrowing.

Endless money printing and borrowing would be every investor's dream! And following our investment strategy described in Chapter 6 would make you even more money than just following the stock market.

You will not lose out in any way by following our advice if the future is a long-term bull market with no serious inflation.

But what if massive money printing and borrowing does, in fact, eventually cause inflation?

This clearly is not an academic question. It's a real-life decision.

Our view is that it is so tempting to keep printing money, and the alternative is so economically terrible, that our government will decide to keep printing. And, by the time we finally stop printing due to very high inflation and interest rates, it will be too late to keep asset prices up at anything close to where they are today.

In that case, following the investment strategy described in Chapter 6 will also make you lots of money – **much, MUCH more than not following it.**

So, either way, whether we are right or wrong about Fake Money, we've designed a way to come out ahead.

How much more money can the Fed print before it creates asset-bubble-popping inflation and interest rates? We don't know for sure.

What we do know for sure is that we are about to find out!

EPILOGUE
It's Productivity Growth, Stupid!

"It's the economy, stupid!" was a popular mantra during the 1992 presidential election between Bill Clinton and George Bush. Bill Clinton's political adviser, James Carville, made that comment in an interview to highlight what he thought was the big issue of the campaign. Clearly, he thought the issue would help Mr. Clinton win. And it probably did. We were in the midst of a minor recession and people were not happy about it. They wanted a change.

The Covid recession had far worse repercussions. The mantra today could be, "It's government stimulus, stupid!" as the pressure became enormous on both Republicans and Democrats to spend lots of borrowed and printed Fake Money.

Of course, that will boost the economy – for a while. As this book points out, this massive increase in Fake Money will help the economy . . . until we get inflation. At that point, it's game over. Borrowing and printing more Fake Money will no longer work, and the negative consequences of all our past printing and borrowing will be devastating.

So, what do we do then?

It's a complex question with an easy answer: *We increase productivity.*

As we have detailed in all our *Aftershock* books, increasing productivity is the *only* way to create real increases in income, generating *real* not Fake Money and real wealth.

Hence, we are making a clarion call to all economists, liberal and conservative, to focus their efforts on the issue of *increasing productivity.*

Currently, there are few economists who are seriously championing the importance of productivity growth. Robert Gordon, from Northwestern University is one of them. In 2016, he wrote a lengthy and important book on the subject, *The Rise and Fall of American Growth: The US Standard of Living since the Civil War.* Unfortunately, at the age of 80, he is probably nearing the end of his career, just when we need him the most.

Not that there aren't other economists working on productivity growth, but not to any great effect on the profession. In fact, most economists tend to ignore productivity beyond discussing the government figures on productivity growth, which barely reflect real increases in productivity.

Instead, liberal economists tend to focus more on the *distribution* of wealth and income. Hence, their interests are in progressive taxation, increasing the minimum wage, and providing public services for the poor and middle class, such as publicly funded education and health care. Because they are not very focused on the *creation* of wealth, there is little interest in productivity growth, which is the core (and only) source of wealth and income creation.

The liberal economists very much reflect a view that would be appropriate in an older agricultural economy where there is a limited amount of agricultural land owned by an inherited family. In that environment, there is a fixed amount of wealth and the only question is how to divide it. In the modern era, the amount of wealth is in no way fixed. Instead, wealth can grow enormously through *productivity growth,* such as the application of machines to farming.

Nonetheless, many liberal economists and many conservative economists tend to view increases in wealth as dependent on control of more land and resources. That is increasingly wrong in the modern industrial and trade-oriented economies that dominate today's world.

Interestingly, liberal economists' interest in, and support of, strong publicly funded education is the single most important driver of productivity growth. Co-author Dr. David Wiedemer was highly unusual in focusing on this key element of public education when he did his dissertation on the return on investment to public education from 1870 to 1970. Public education has been critically important to increasing US productivity. Our nation's focus on public education is one of the reasons our economy has consistently outperformed most economies in the rest of the world.

Yet, that key aspect of education – its importance in driving productivity growth – is often *not* the focus of liberal economists. They are more focused on its role in reducing inequality. And the efficiency and productivity of producing public education is not their focus.

Education and health care are the two parts of the economy most desperately in need of productivity improvement. While manufacturing has seen big increases in productivity over the past 50 years, both education and health care have seen big decreases in productivity, which have offset the productivity increases in manufacturing. The lack of increased productivity in education and health care is the key reason they have become such a large part of the economy.

Liberal economists also lack the focus on productivity growth that is desperately needed to improve poor and middle-class living standards. For liberals, this is an especially huge failure.

Unfortunately, this failure is matched, to a large degree, by conservative economists. Although there is more focus on productivity growth by conservative economists (they tend to be more business focused), it is often not as high a priority for them as limiting government services and transfer payments to people with lower incomes.

Although the level of government services and related taxation are important economic issues, like wealth distribution, they are not that critical to productivity growth. For example, one of our highest periods of productivity growth was in the 1950s and 1960s. During that period, we also had one of our highest levels of income taxation in history – top tax levels were 90% in the 1950s and only fell to 70% in the 1960s. That period also saw an extremely large increase in the amount and breadth of government services – educational services as well as new programs designed to help lower-income groups, such as Medicare, Medicaid, food stamps, Aid to Families with Dependent Children, and many other smaller programs.

We are not advocating high taxes. The point of this example is that neither high taxes nor high levels of government services had much of an impact on productivity growth. Creating the right taxation system and determining the proper amount of government services is part of productivity growth, but it is hardly the key, as the 1950s and 1960s show. *Significant productivity growth depends on factors that are much, much more fundamental.*

Exactly what we should do to increase productivity would take more than a simple epilogue to explain. In fact, it would take a whole book, or series of books. However, what we can say in an epilogue is that one of the first and most important changes needed to increase productivity would be to drastically reduce stock and real estate prices. High-priced stocks and high-priced real estate don't help productivity growth in any way. They also make the changes needed for real productivity growth politically impossible.

Of course, there is absolutely no support for drastically reducing stock and real estate prices – in fact, just the opposite. Most of our country's economic focus will be on doing everything we can to maintain high stock and real estate prices, including printing massive amounts of Fake Money. That will eventually devastate those high stock and real estate prices, as well as the entire economy.

We'd be better off pulling the plug on it now and focusing on productivity growth as soon as possible. That won't happen, of course. Instead, we are headed toward a huge bubble pop that Fake Money will no longer be able to fix.

The economic and human suffering will be rough. But there is an upside to the coming devastation. It sets the stage for the changes needed for massive productivity growth. It is the platinum lining to the dark cloud of the Aftershock!

At that point, all economic hands on deck!!! Those few economists who still have jobs (and even those who don't), whether they be liberal or conservative or something in between, need to seize the moment and focus night and day on improving productivity. The sooner the better, because we will be in real pain.

We haven't had any big improvements in productivity since the 1960s. There were massive improvements in the productivity of manufacturing computers, but that didn't translate into big productivity improvements for some of its biggest users, such as health care, the government, and education. It's a great example of increases in manufacturing productivity being offset by decreases in service sector productivity.

The Aftershock will blow the cover off that sad fact when the Fake Money bubbles burst. It won't be a pretty picture. But the long-term future will be a beautiful picture, once we take the time and effort to focus on *productivity improvement.*

Economists can and should try to make a huge improvement in our daily living standards. At the University of Wisconsin, it's called the Wisconsin Idea. That idea is that university research should be applied to solve problems and improve the health, quality of life, and the environment for all citizens of the state and, ultimately, the country.

The Wisconsin Idea should drive all economists to focus on improving productivity. Those economists who help solve the productivity problems will certainly be one of the greatest generations of economists ever.

APPENDIX

A

Buying Stock Is Not Investing

Buying stocks has less to do with actual investing than you might think. Actual investing means actually giving money to a company to grow its business. That's not only our definition of investing, it is also almost every economist's definition of investing.

Among academic or government economists producing the economic reports so closely watched by Wall Street, business investment is always defined as the actual use of money to grow a business. That could be investments in new computers, a factory, an office building a warehouse, research, employee training, marketing, and so on.

What would never be considered investment by almost any economist is Warren Buffett or any other "investor" buying the stock of Burlington Northern Railroad. Once the initial stock offering is complete and stocks are bought and sold on a stock exchange, "investors" are simply trading stocks among themselves. After the initial IPO, no additional money goes to the Burlington Northern Railroad or any other company that has issued stock.

Warren Buffett Is Not a Great Investor, He's a Great Stock Picker

Warren Buffett isn't investing. He's not a great investor, or even a so-so investor. He makes money trading stocks. He is a great stock picker.

Unlike Buffett, an example of a great investor would be A.P. Giannini, who founded Bank of America. He invested the money he made from a fruit supply business in San Francisco (along with some money from other people) into starting Bank of America from scratch and building it into the largest bank in the world.

Now, that's investing! It produced enormous profits and wealth. That's what builds a real economy. But it takes a lot of skill and enormous perseverance. Honestly, what Warren Buffett does really doesn't help the economy much at all.

Buying Stock from Peter and Transferring It to Paul Is Not Investing

Instead, this is called buying stock on the secondary market. That means you aren't investing in the company, you are just helping Peter to liquidate his stock and then you are selling it to Paul. There is almost no investment value to that transaction. Yes, providing a highly liquid secondary market in which stockholders can easily sell their stock is a useful function, but it is hardly investing.

True, investing in the first sale of stock in an initial public offering is investing. But those transactions represent a very, very small part of stock market activity. Also, buying a secondary offering is a direct investment, but that too represents a very small part of the market.

The reality is that large corporations don't rely at all on the stock market for investment. They rely on banks or go directly to the bond markets and issue corporate bonds to raise the money they need for investment. Many of the smaller NASDAQ companies cannot issue corporate bonds, but they do have banking relationships for loans and have other ways to raise debt financing, such as junk bonds.

The stock market is simply not where companies go to raise money for investing in their business.

All of this is true in both a bubble and a non-bubble stock market. So why does this distinction matter more in a bubble market like today's record-high markets?

Because Buying Stock Is Not Investing; Stock Prices Don't Necessarily Depend on the Company's Financial Performance

The clear disconnect between buying stocks and investing makes it very easy for the stock market to be disconnected from bad financial realities of companies. Those bad financial realities can be internal, in the form of a bad product, or external, in the form of a bad economy. Either way, stocks can keep going up, as long as "investors" continue to buy from Peter and sell to Paul.

For example, if you are investing in a company by lending it money, you expect to be paid back all your money plus interest. To do that, the company's financial realities, in terms of profits and revenues, have to be good enough to pay that money back. The company's financial realities, therefore, are very important to its ability to pay off its debt.

However, if Peter buys IBM stock from Paul, the company has no requirement to perform for Peter. It doesn't have to be well-enough managed to pay back debt and interest. The value of the investment is entirely dependent on how much Peter is willing to pay Paul. Yes, the way Peter values the stock may be related to IBM's revenues and profits, but it doesn't have to be.

In fact, in a bubble stock market, it can be wildly different. That's why we call it a bubble. And, that's part of the thrill of stock investing in a bubble – the value of the stock can become very disconnected from reality in a very positive way for the investor. In fact, the more disconnected from reality it becomes, the better it is for the investor.

As long as lots of other "investors" try to disconnect themselves from reality, the stock market can become a massive instant wealth-creation machine – until it pops. The bubble can keep going strong for a long time, depending on the depth of the disconnect from reality – the depth of the delusion.

That's what gave us the Covid-19 recession stock boom – something that we have seen for many years in the stock market, just much, much more. More disconnection, more delusion, more denial.

That the stock market hit record highs in the midst of a massive recession is not really a mystery. That it continues to set new highs as we exit the recession and deal with the repercussions of trillions in stimulus money is not incomprehensible, either. It's just another level up in the market distancing itself from reality.

To avoid the obvious and deny the deeply critical reasoning just described for why the Covid-19 recession stock boom is happening, you will see almost everyone giving you another reason – any reason, other than the real reason. That includes liberal economists like Paul Krugman, who explains that the stock market is high because there is no good alternative to buying stocks. A Merrill Lynch salesperson could easily give you the same explanation. Or other market commentators and participants could give you a million other explanations.

The only explanation you won't see very often is that this stock market boom is just a further movement away from reality – a reality we have been running away from for many, many years.

Before a Bubble Market Pops, an Increasing Disconnect from Reality Is Hugely Profitable

"All the investments I made money on I bought at too high a price."

Figure A.1   NASDAQ 100 January 2, 1980, to June 30, 2021.

Source: NASDAQ.

Disconnecting from reality can be wildly profitable. The stock market has been the greatest source of wealth creation in our history. It will also be the greatest source of wealth destruction in our history when the disconnect from reality dies.

It's hard to find a more succinct description of success in a bubble economy than that. Even if you buy at too high a price, it will be valued at an even higher price down the road, assuming the bubble continues.

For the last 40 years, the stock bubble has continued (Figure A.1). It's been the greatest source of wealth creation in our history. It will also be the greatest source of wealth destruction in our history, but it sure feels good while it lasts!

In a Real Market and Real Economy, Disconnecting from Reality Is Disastrous

If you are trying to make money the old-fashioned way – by making a profit – any disconnect from reality can spell disaster for your company and its profits. Same for an individual. Same for the economy. If you can't see reality, you are guaranteed to eventually crash and burn.

By the way, that's why Henry Ford was so reluctant to sell stock in his company. He was in a real economy and a real stock market. He didn't want to share the enormous profits from Ford Motor. He would try to borrow instead or find other ways to get money that didn't involve giving away profits or giving away control of his company.

But in a bubble market, the money is made by selling stock at very high prices to investors – prices that are far higher than could ever be supported by company profits. The more stock you can sell at high prices, the more money you make.

Bubble Markets and Economies Always Become Real at Some Point

The fun disconnected from reality cannot last forever. Why? Well, that's reality! If we could avoid reality forever, that means there is no reality, which isn't reality, even though many on Wall Street and the government think so.

More specifically, reality will hit *when significant inflation hits,* as explained in Chapter 3. When one person heard about this book's title, *Fake Money, Real Danger,* he said, "There's a lot of truth in those words." We might add, there's a whole lot of *reality.*

APPENDIX B

The Trouble with Bubbles

ROBERT WIEDEMER

Summary: **The shale oil and gas boom and bust is a microcosm of why bubbles feel so good on the way up and are so devastating on the way down.**

If you want to know what it looks like when our big Fake Money bubble pops, you could have no better guide than to look at the shale oil and gas industry.

I grew up in the oil and gas industry in New Mexico and Texas. And, unlike many people, I loved it. Not so much the big oil corporations, but the small, independent oil and gas producers. It was an amazing and interesting group of people and a truly exciting business – in both good and bad ways. My father was one of those independent drillers and producers.

I know the oil and gas industry well. Everything from researching potential oil and gas drilling sites to drilling, fracking, and production. I literally have seen or done it all.

Although you may not follow the oil and gas industry the way I do, you have undoubtedly heard about the shale oil and gas boom. The boom was often referred to as the *fracking revolution* and is known for both its environmental controversy as well as the incredible amounts of oil and gas it produced.

And what a production boom it was! US oil production rose from 5 million barrels a day to over 13 million barrels a day, making the US the largest oil producer in the world.

Natural gas production exploded to 100 billion cubic feet a day in 2019, up from 55 billion in 1995. The price of natural gas fell from as high as $15 per thousand cubic feet in 2005 to just $1.50 per thousand cubic feet in 2020.

Low-priced natural gas began to power more and more electricity generation, ultimately displacing coal as the primary fuel source for electricity generation. It made the US a net natural gas exporter after years of being a net gas importer from Canada. The gas industry developed massive liquefied natural gas terminals on the Atlantic Ocean and Gulf Coast to export natural gas as a liquid all around the world.

Cheap gas also made possible an explosion of petrochemical production (mostly plastics). In fact, the biggest construction project in the United States in 2020 was a plastics plant outside of Pittsburgh that will use cheap natural gas from the nearby Marcellus gas shale region as feedstock.

Only One "Small" Problem with Booming Shale Oil and Natural Gas: Absolutely No Profit

That's right, nobody made a single dime off of producing shale oil and gas. The only way they made money was through the rising value of the stock of shale oil and gas companies or the rising value of shale oil and gas properties.

No money was ever made off the actual sale of the oil and gas itself. Ever.

Drilling and producing shale oil and gas is very expensive. Shale companies never made money on oil production even when oil was at $100 a barrel. As the price of oil came down, shale companies were able to drastically lower their costs, but never enough to make a profit.

Natural gas was even worse. As the boom got going, prices declined – and kept declining. There was never a period when shale gas companies made money selling natural gas.

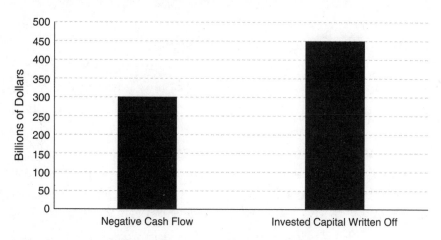

Figure B.1   Shale Industry Losses over the Past 15 Years

Source: Deloitte.

Although a lot of money was made in the oil and gas shale industry over the last 15 years, almost all of it was from the sale of stock or land. However, according to Big 4 accounting firm Deloitte, the operating losses were enormous. Stock and land prices are now increasingly reflecting the reality of no operating profits.

The monetary losses have been horrible. In 2019, a *research report prepared by Big 4 accounting firm, Deloitte, concluded that the shale industry peaked without ever making money.* The report said that over the past decade and a half, the shale industry totaled $300 billion in net negative cash flow. In addition, the shale industry wrote down another $450 billion in invested capital and saw more than 190 bankruptcies since 2010 (Figure B.1).

In other words, the whole thing – *all of it* – was a big fat stock and land bubble.

For Many, the Bubble Was Wonderful

The shale oil and natural gas boom made a few billionaires and many, many millionaires. It created high-paying jobs for hundreds of thousands of white-collar AND blue-collar jobs directly. Indirectly, it drove the creation of hundreds of thousands of more high-paying blue-collar and white-collar jobs in supporting industries.

The massive related booms in petrochemicals, liquefied natural gas, and oil and gas pipelines created jobs for huge numbers of people, much of it in manufacturing and construction.

Best of all, almost all these high-paying jobs were created in the USA.

What could be better?!

So What If It Was All a Big Bubble?

This is an important question. Who cares if it's a bubble? Look at all the money people made and all the incredible jobs it created! Weren't there a lot of great benefits?

This is the same question we can ask, not only about the shale oil and gas bubble, but about any of our current financial bubbles driven by fake money. What is so bad about a bubble that makes so many people rich and others gainfully employed?

Because the bubble pops.

Drilling for oil and gas collapsed in 2019. From a high of almost 1100 rigs at the end of 2018, the number of rigs drilling for oil and gas fell to 244 in August 2020.

And like many bubbles recently, this bubble has rebounded with the Covid pandemic. Despite big reductions in worldwide demand, shale drilling increased with the stock market. Saudi Arabia and Russia also helped the drilling rebound immensely with major cuts in oil production, which kept the price of oil from collapsing. The rig count increased from that low of 244 in August 2020 to almost 500 as of summer 2021.

And, as of summer 2021 a lot of that demand for oil is coming back pushing the price of oil over $70. More importantly, the stock market is still growing, so shale drilling will likely increase further. Will it go back to its high of 1100 a few years ago? Unlikely.

More importantly, will it make money? Actually, it might finally make some money. Some industry analysts predict the shale industry will actually see positive cash flow of $50 billion in 2022. But, that would hardly offset the massive past losses and is not guaranteed. Oil industry analysts have been over optimistic about shale profitability for 15 years now. It's unlikely that is over now.

That's because the fundamental problem is that shale oil and gas drilling doesn't make money. It's expensive. It is not a technological revolution. There was no such thing as a "fracking revolution" that dramatically lowered the costs of oil and gas drilling.

In fact, every well drilled in the US and almost everywhere else in the world since 1950 has been hydraulically fracked. It's not a new technology at all.

As a college student, I went to a fracking operation in the early 1980s. It's an amazing operation to watch with lots of high-powered equipment, but hydraulic fracking wasn't at all new then. It was done all the time. And it isn't at all new now. The technology has been improved since the 1980s, but it had been improving dramatically since the 1950s. Fracking has seen continuous improvement for decades, but no revolution.

Even horizontal drilling, which is the key to unlocking shale oil, wasn't new. It was widely used in offshore drilling in the 1980s. Its use for onshore drilling is new, and it the closest thing to a technological revolution, but it isn't a cost-reducing revolution. It's simply applying a very, very costly undersea drilling technology to use onshore.

The "fracking revolution" was bubble hype. It wasn't real. Yes, the money all those people made along the way could buy real things. But it wasn't based on profits from selling oil and gas. It was based on profits from selling stock and land. It's just another part of the broader stock and real estate bubble. The "fracking revolution" was just a way to hype shale oil and gas stock and real estate. Eventually, the "fracking revolution" stock and real estate bubble eventually collapses. All the money disappears, as do all the jobs.

We haven't seen a complete collapse in the shale industry yet, but much of it already has collapsed. If shale oil and gas made money on producing oil and gas, it wouldn't be a bubble and could come back stronger than ever before. But since it never did make any money and likely won't make much money in the future, it is simply a stock and real estate bubble that will pop along with the broader stock and real estate bubble.

In the end, bubbles produce far more losses than gains.

The Trouble with Bubbles

Until the shale oil and gas bubble fully pops, some people will say it will come back because they don't realize (or don't want to realize) that it's a bubble. Bubbles are hard to see for people who are benefiting from them – until they pop.

Therein lies the trouble with the bubbles we have today. They feel great while they last, but they are fake, and when they pop, all the good stuff goes and all that is left is misery and no rebound at all.

We will also realize we never should have pumped up those bubbles, whether it be in oil shale or, much more importantly, in the stock, bond, and real estate markets, and the economy.

But our troubles don't end there. The even bigger problem with bubbles is that when the fake money is lost, it takes a lot of very real money with it. Lots and lots of real money.

So, you are far, far worse off than before the bubbles were created. The economy and stock markets will be far worse off than they were at the start of the 1980s, before the bubbles began.

Will the economy go back to the 1950s standard of living? It could. It all depends on how much fake money we create before it all pops. *The more we create now, the further the bubble pop pushes the economy back in time – maybe to the living standards we had before the 1950s.*

Of course, we will learn from this. Once the bubbles pop, we will never allow it to happen again. All future growth will be based on productivity growth, not bubble growth. After paying such a heavy price, the US public will be deathly afraid of allowing or supporting any bubbles in the future.

Right now, you couldn't have a better view of the future of our fake money bubbles than to look at the shale oil and gas industry today.

PS: The World Will Not Run Out of Oil

Unlike in the US, drilling in the Middle East isn't slowing down as much, and there is tons more oil that can be produced in the Middle East. Iran and Iraq have the potential to produce almost as much as Saudi Arabia. Saudi Arabia can drill for more oil, as can Kuwait and the United Arab Emirates. This may be uncomfortable and may not be a good situation from a security standpoint, but that's the economic reality.

More to the point, it is geologic reality. All our cheapest oil has been drilled and produced. That makes sense. Oil companies find and produce the cheapest, most profitable oil first, and we've been drilling and producing oil and gas in the U.S. far longer than the people in the Middle East. Plus, many of their formations have more oil than US oil formations.

However, let's be clear, the US still has massive amounts of oil that could be produced both offshore and onshore; it's just not as cheap to produce as it was earlier. Middle East oil will be cheaper to produce than US oil for years to come.

And it's not just the US being affected. North Sea oil will also get crushed. Canada oil sands will be crushed. Argentinian oil shale already has been crushed. Older oil fields in Mexico and Nigeria will become increasingly less productive, even if those countries take actions to increase their oil fields' longevity.

Mideast oil will become more and more dominant if economics is the only issue. Clearly, the US could subsidize oil shale to help us remain free from oil imports from the Middle East. Or we could just ban the import of Mideast oil, which would be much easier and less costly. Much, if not most, of our oil imports often come from outside the Middle East anyway.

APPENDIX C

An Important Long-Term Lack of Correlation

ROBERT WIEDEMER

Summary: People often assume that movements in the price of gold reflect movements in the value of the dollar. They don't. Same for the price of stocks and news events.

One of my friends who likes gold (I have many friends who do) was asking me about the movements in gold over the summer of 2020. He said several times that he thought the upward movements might be due to a falling US dollar. And, conversely, downward movements were due, in part, to a rising US dollar.

This is a common belief. I hear it on the business news shows all the time.

However, I was pretty sure it was wrong. Gold had been rising rapidly for more than a year (it was up more than 50%), and I knew the dollar hadn't fallen anywhere near 50%. Any correlation between the two was likely to be small. Although any daily price movement in gold might be attributable to a falling or rising dollar, I thought it was more of an excuse for why gold was rising, rather than a real reason.

I told my friend that, honestly, I thought gold was rising because psychology had become more positive on gold. Just as stocks had risen in the period between late March and June 2020 largely on psychology, not on any great news for stocks.

People hate it when I tell them that psychology is the primary driver of stock prices day to day and for gold prices, as well. They don't want to feel like the market is driven so heavily by psychology. Of course, they know psychology plays a role, but they're much more comfortable about their investments in gold or stock if they can base it on some kind of tangible and logical reasoning.

I would add that I think they also feel more comfortable with the world in general if stocks and other investments are driven by tangibles, and not simply by psychology.

I certainly understand the need for feeling that investment prices are driven by tangible reasons. It makes it easier to evaluate investments, it makes sense, and it makes investors feel more comfortable that they have made the right investment.

But my intuition remained the same. I suspected that if I looked at the correlation between the dollar and gold, I would find very little.

Sure enough, when I created a chart correlating the price of gold with movements in the dollar, I found almost no correlation, as Figures C.1 and C.2 indicate.

Figure C.1   Changes in the Value of the Dollar (DXY) from January 2, 2011, to June 30, 2021

Source: Standard & Poor's.

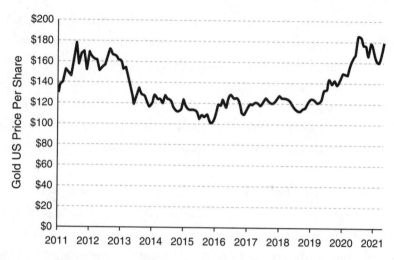

Figure C.2   Changes in the Value of Gold (GLD) from January 2, 2011, to June 30, 2021

Source: Standard & Poor's.

For the last decade, the dollar (based on DXY, a basket of foreign currencies) has moved up and down, but its up-and-down movements don't correlate at all with the price of gold.

Not that there aren't fundamental forces at work driving gold, but they are very different and much more scary than simple movements in the dollar. What's driving gold is that some investors are feeling we are in a bubble market driven by federal government stimulus that is sure to fail eventually. Hence, it is not at all surprising that when the first big bubble market failed, the dot-com bubble, that gold began its long-term bull market. It has far outperformed stocks since then, even when including dividends for stocks.

Sure, it took a massive hit when many investors thought the worst was behind us in 2013, but over time, it became obvious that the fundamental problems of massive money printing and borrowing were not behind us, but have only gotten worse. Hence, gold recovered most of its losses. It will go well beyond that. When? It's hard to say.

What is easy to say is that its rise won't be correlated to relatively small movements in the dollar. Some people would say that gold is inherently a psychological investment because it does not produce any income that can be valued. Stocks can be more easily valued based on the earnings they produce. There is some of truth to that. But, in the current market, I suspected there wasn't much truth to that.

I looked at two different stocks and the correlation of earnings to movements in their stock price. The stocks were Walmart (Figures C.3 and C.4) and McDonald's (Figures C.5 and C.6). They are companies whose earnings, and not hype, should drive their stock prices.

And news, either corporate or economic, should drive their earnings. I don't have a simple way to quantify the number and importance of news events. However, because any important news should affect earnings, I am using earnings as a measure of news.

Hence, if there is a series of bad news events, it will cause a series of downward changes in earnings, and the price of the stock should reflect that by going down. On the other hand, if there is a series of good news events, it will cause a series of upward changes in earnings, and the price of the stock should reflect that by going up.

However, that's not how the charts look at all. Instead, the price of both stocks over the last decade move with little relation to earnings changes. That means these stock prices have little relation to news events (Figures C.3 – C.6).

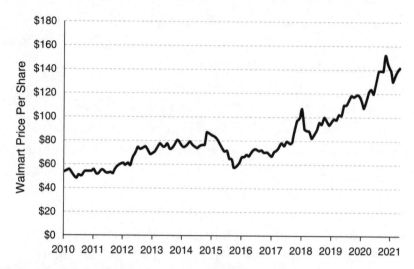

Figure C.3   Changes in the Value of Walmart's Stock from January 2010 to June 30, 2021

Source: Standard & Poor's.

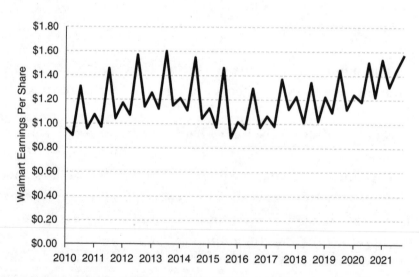

Figure C.4   Changes in Walmart's Quarterly Earnings per Share from January 2010 to June 30, 2021

Source: Walmart.

Figure C.5   Changes in the Value of McDonald's Stock from January 2010 to June 30, 2021

Source: Standard & Poor's.

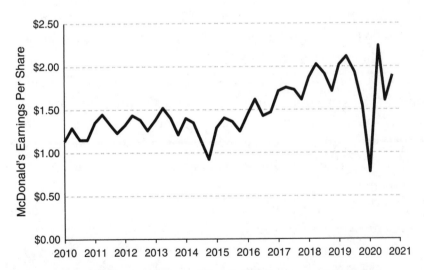

Figure C.6   Changes in McDonald's Quarterly Earnings per Share from January 2010 to June 30, 2021

Source: McDonald's.

For the last decade, there has been little correlation between changes in earnings, which should reflect important news events, and changes in Walmart's stock price. Likewise, for the last decade, there has been little correlation between changes in earnings, which should reflect important news events, and changes in McDonald's stock price.

Given these facts, I have to conclude that economic news or specific company news has little long-term impact on a company's stock price.

So, when you hear commentators try to tell you "why" stock prices are going up or down, the reasons they are giving you are almost always wrong. In fact, as the charts show, the movement in stock prices over the last 10 years is much more related to investor psychology than it is to any news.

Analysts and business news commentators are essentially just making up stories about why any given news is affecting stock prices. They make up these stories to make investors feel better. Whether it is bad news affecting a stock's price or good news, the key is that there is always some rational reason for stocks to move up or down. That makes investors feel better when stocks are going up – and especially when they are going down – because it all seems rational, maybe even predictable.

"It's not just based on psychology," these analysts would say. Stock price movements are based on solid and important news facts.

But, it is clear from the charts above that that it is absolutely untrue.

People don't want to think that the investing world is nuts. What does that say about the future value of their investments? What does that say about the best and brightest people on Wall Street and academia? What does that say about the future of our economy and the world's economy? Well, nothing good, certainly. Facing that reality is unsettling to everyone, for obvious reasons.

Our New Model Reveals Why the Stock Market Bubble Is So Hard to See – And How It Will Likely Pop

The central idea of this book is that the stock, bond, and real estate markets have been in a bubble for years, and now the government's massive stimulus (money printing and borrowing) in response to the Covid Crisis has put us on a faster track to the inevitable big bubble pop ahead, especially for the stock market.

However, most investors and stock analysts do not think we are in a bubble. That's partially because they don't want to see it. But there's more to it than that. Unlike most bubbles in the past, this stock market bubble has been driven by *multiple components* that, individually, are hard to see – and that makes the overall bubble hard to see, as well

To make these various components easier to see, we have created a financial model that sheds light on how much each component contributes to the growth of the stock market bubble. This analytical model was designed by coauthor David Wiedemer, PhD, Economics, University of Wisconsin – Madison.

Before Dr. Wiedemer designed our Bubble Insight Model, we assumed that the stock market bubble, like most asset bubbles, was mostly the result of "Animal Spirits" – meaning very positive, at times even euphoric, investor psychology that over time pushes stock prices higher and higher.

Of course, we also knew that other factors, such as economic growth and corporate earnings, also play important roles. But we thought that, just like most bubbles in the past, this bubble was primarily being driven upward by powerful Animal Spirits.

Turns out, we were wrong.

Our data-driven Bubble Insight Model showed us that the biggest driver of the huge stock market bubble is not at all what we originally thought. While the influence of Animal

Spirits is certainly important, this time we have a much more powerful bubble booster – and future bubble buster – driving the market.

The Bubble Insight Model Illuminates What's Hard to See

Our model has surprised us in many ways. First, as already mentioned, we discovered that the impact of Animal Spirits (positive investor psychology) does not account for most of the relentless rise of today's stock market bubble.

We also learned that the contributions to stock market growth made by rising economic growth and rising corporate profits – both typically assumed to be key drivers of stock market growth – turned out to be quite modest.

All of these components are playing some role in pushing up the market, but none of the usual suspects turned out to be the most dominant driver of the rising stock market bubble for the last four decades.

Our model made its determinations by assessing each component's individual growth and then calculating each component's relative contribution to the huge rise of the stock market over the last four decades. What we found is shown in Figure D.1.

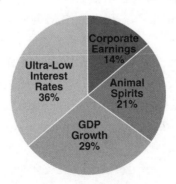

Figure D.1 Key Drivers of the Rising Stock Market Bubble, 1980–2021

As you can see from the pie chart above, our model shows that the biggest factor pushing up the stock market since 1980 is falling interest rates. Not economic growth. Not rising corporate profits. Not even spunky Animal Spirits (the usual cause of most asset bubbles). Surprisingly, falling interest rates trumps all of these, with the largest relative contribution to the overall rise of the market.

We always knew that interest rates were important. In fact, all our earlier books predicted that *rising* interest rates would ultimately bring the bubbles down. But until we had the Bubble Insight Model, we had no idea just how much *falling* interest rates helped drive up the stock market bubble.

Now we know exactly how much: 36%.

Not only does our model establish that falling interest rates were more responsible for pushing up the stock market bubble than any other contributing driver, the model also confirms that the opposite will occur: rising interest rates will be the dominant force that pulls the stock market bubble down.

What will drive interest rates up?

How high will interest rates go before the stock market significantly falls?

When will the bubble pop?

And how low will the market fall?

All these questions, and more, are exactly what our model is designed to answer.

And in case you might be thinking all this math stuff is not for you, we have some good news. Without having to understand any equations or formulas behind the model, you – and anyone who visits the book's website at www.FakeMoneyReal Danger.com/model – can enter whatever numbers you please into our interactive model and see for yourself how it could affect the stock market, what could burst the bubble, and when it could pop.

For now, while you are still reading the book and not yet playing with our Bubble Insight Model online, let's walk through how the model can illuminate the hidden components of this hard-to-see bubble – and also see how it will likely pop, causing massive loss of wealth for those who are not paying attention.

Our guess is, if you are reading this Appendix, you certainly are paying attention!

Let's begin now by looking at how the stock market exploded in growth from the 1980s to today.

How Did the Stock Market Bubble Grow So Big?

Our model can show you the answer. But first, a bit of background.

Way back in the 1970s, before the rise of the current stock market bubble, interest rates were high due to high inflation. In an effort to lower inflation, the Federal Reserve raised interest rates even further in the late 1970s and early 1980s by greatly reducing its purchases of bonds (money printing).

The big decrease in money printing reduced inflation. As inflation fell, the Fed was able to slowly reduce interest rates by slowly increasing the amount of money it printed. Also helping reduce interest rates further during that time was a massive increase in purchases of US bonds by foreign investors.

As a result of slowly decreasing interest rates staying relatively low, the federal government was able to borrow (and spend) increasingly larger amounts of money. This helped bring us out of the early 1980s recession and launched the beginnings of the huge financial bubbles we have today, including the stock market bubble.

That is the story of how the bubbles began to grow, but the model looks more closely at all the factors driving up the stock market.

Analyzing historical data from 1980 to 2021, our model looked at all the major factors. However, before we start looking at the contributing factors, we first need to know how much the stock market has grown since 1980.

The numbers are shocking.

How Much Did the Dow Grow Since 1980?

Dow in 1980	Dow in 2021	Growth Factor
1,000	35,000	35

Our model shows that the Dow Jones Industrial Average exploded from about 1,000 in 1980 to more than 35,000 in 2021.

That's a *35-fold increase!*

Many people assume this explosive growth of the market since 1980 must have resulted from equally explosive economic and corporate earnings growth.

But is that true? Let's use the model to find out.

How Much of the Growth of the Dow Is Due to Economic Growth?

Economic growth certainly played an important role in the Dow's stunning rise. But how much did GDP growth actually contribute?

In the last four decades, GDP rose from about $3.2 trillion in 1980 to roughly $21.5 trillion in 2021. That's a 6.7 fold increase!

But it's nowhere near as big as the 35-fold increase of the Dow. That means the 6.7 fold increase in economic growth contributed **only about 19%** to the huge 35 fold rise of the Dow (Why? Because 6.7 is 19% of 35).

How Much Did GDP Growth Contribute to the Growth of the Dow?

GDP in 1980	GDP in 2021	Growth Factor	Contribution of GDP Growth to the Growth of the Dow
$3.2 trillion	$21.5 trillion	6.7	19%

This is truly unexpected. Most people (including us) would have thought the contribution of rising GDP played a bigger role. But the numbers don't lie. It's only 19%

However, the story doesn't end there. We also need to look at GDP adjusted for inflation.

GDP Growth Adjusted for Inflation

Inflation rates are always changing, so our model uses averages. From 1980 to 2021, inflation rose an average of 3% per year – a very modest annual rate. However, after it is compounded over 41 years, inflation grew a total of 326% since 1980.

How much did inflation contribute to GDP growth? Since inflation increased by 326%, then about 49% of the GDP's 670% growth since 1980 was due to inflation. (Why? Because 326 is 49% of 670.)

How Much Did Inflation Contribute to GDP Growth?

1980	2021	Percent Increase	Contribution of Inflation to GDP Growth
Avg. inflation rate of 3% per year		326%	49%

The fact that 49% of GDP growth since 1980 has been due to inflation means that *almost half* of GDP growth during this time was not "real" economic growth and, therefore, should be ignored.

So instead of thinking that economic growth was key to the rise of the stock market during all these years, our model helps us see that, in fact, the growth of the economy played a much smaller role in pushing the stock bubble up than most people may realize.

Economic Growth Played a Relatively Small Role in Driving Up the Stock Market

So far, our Bubble Insight Model has determined that economic growth contributed no more than 19% to the huge rise of the stock market since 1980.

However, when adjusted for inflation, the real economy grew only half as much. Which means real economic growth contributed, not 19%, but *less than 10%*, to the growth of the Dow.

Wow, that's low. Without our analytical model, we certainly would not have guessed that. Would you?

If the rising stock market is not being driven heavily by economic growth, what else has been pushing stocks higher?

Most people assume that, along with economic growth, rising corporate profits are also responsible for pushing up the market.

But did corporate profits rise enough to explain a 35-fold increase in the Dow?

Let's use our model to determine how much rising corporate profits have contributed to the huge rise of the Dow from 1980 to 2021.

How Much of the Huge Growth of the Dow Is Due to Rising Corporate Profits?

Rising corporate profits help drive up stock prices. After all, a share of a company's stock gives an investor the right to a share of the company's profits. Therefore, stock prices tend to rise as company profits rise.

Typically, corporate profits increase over time at about the same rate that GDP increases. However, corporate profits, as a percent of GDP, tend to be higher during an economic boom and lower during an economic recession.

In other words, when compared to GDP growth, corporate profits rise faster than GDP growth in good times, and they rise slower than GDP growth in bad times. And, as you would expect, this difference impacts the growth of the stock market.

In the last 40 years, how much did rising corporate profits, as a percentage of GDP, contribute to the huge rise of the Dow?

Corporate profits increased from 6% of GDP in 1980 to 9% of GDP in 2021. That's a 50% increase.

But remember, the stock market had a whopping 3500% increase since 1980. That means rising corporate profits contributed only about 14% to the total growth of the Dow.

How Much Did Rising Corporate Profits Contribute to the Growth of the Dow?

1980	2021	Growth Factor	Contribution of Rising Corporate Profits to the Growth of the Dow
6.4%	9.6%	1.50	14%

Most people would probably guess that rising corporate profits played a much bigger role in the huge growth of the

Dow. Without a model to objectively analyze it, hardly anyone would have thought its contribution was only 14%.

The model makes it clear that even if we combine **both** corporate profits (about 14% of the Dow's growth) **and** real economic growth (about 10% of the Dow's growth) – long assumed to be the two biggest drivers of stock market growth – the combined impact of both on the rising stock market is less than 25%.

That's just one more well-hidden fact about this hard-to-see stock market bubble that our model helps illuminate.

So, if not economic growth or corporate profit growth, what in the world is the main driver pushing up the Dow?

How Much of the Huge Growth of the Dow Is Due to Falling Interest Rates?

Low interest rates increase the valuation of stocks because they greatly increase the value of future earnings. A simple model for valuing future earnings is a Discounted Cash Flow model. This model values a stream of future earnings over many years.

In this model, even if the future earnings stay the same, the current value of those future earnings goes up dramatically as the current interest rate goes down. **So even if a company's profits or revenues are not growing, the current value of those earnings explodes if interest rates go down.**

The only thing the stock market likes better than low interest rates is *ultra-low* interest rates. The lower interest rates fall, the hotter the stock market gets.

How much did declining interest rate contribute to the growth of the stock market?

Our model reveals that declining interest rates are the biggest reason the Dow exploded in the last four decades.

Interest rates on corporate bonds fell from an average of 10% in 1980 to just 4% in 2021. That's a XX decline.

Therefore, declining interest rates are responsible for 36% of the increase in the Dow (because XX is 36% of 35).

How Much Did Declining Interest Rates Contribute to the Growth of the Dow?

1980	2021	XXXXXXXX	Growth of the Dow due to Increasing Interest Rates
10%	4%	XX	36%

This is one of the biggest surprises coming out of the Bubble Insight Model. Falling interest rates are the biggest component of the hard-to-see stock market bubble. Compared to all the other factors driving up the stock bubble over many years, falling interest rates have made the biggest contribution to the exploding Dow.

But what about our original best guess, Animal Spirits? How much of a contribution to the stock market bubble did super-positive investor psychology provide?

How Much of the Huge Growth of the Dow Is Due to Animal Spirits?

The Bubble Insight Model determined how much of the explosive 35-fold increase in the Dow is due to economic growth (19%), how much is due to increased corporate earnings (14%), and how much is due to the rocket fuel of falling interest rates (36%).

That leaves the remainder of the Dow's growth – about 21% – due to the bubble-creating power of Animal Spirits.

As mentioned earlier, most asset bubbles are created by Animal Spirits. The more a bubble is primarily driven by Animal Spirits (rather than harder-to-see components, as we have today), the more visible the bubble eventually becomes – and the sooner the bubble pops.

The dot-com bubble of the late 1990s is a good example. At first, the technology stock bubble might have seemed like the real deal (no bubble). But eventually a growing number of people were able to see that profitless tech companies were probably not worth as much as the earlier hyper-excited investors were willing to pay.

Growing awareness that the bubble was a bubble eventually popped the dot-com bubble in early 2000. Investors will continue to buy into a rising visible bubble. But once a visible bubble stops rising and begins to fall, no one wants to be the last one out.

Our current enormous stock market bubble is an entirely different species. As our model reveals, its various components (in surprising proportions) are not at all easy to see – and that helps keep the bubble afloat. Instead of investors rushing out and staying out when the bubble declines, enough investors buy the dips to push the bubble market back up. Of course, massive bubble support from the Fed's huge money printing and the Congress' huge borrowing helps enormously to keep the bubble moving up.

Altogether, these factors have created a new species of bionic bubble – a bubble so big and seemingly unpoppable that at times it feels invincible. But even a bionic bubble is still a bubble. And bubbles always eventually pop.

In this particular bubble, the fact that the gigantic stock bubble is so hard to see, coupled with the obvious reality that no one wants to see it means we are in for quite a ride. Especially so, since the government is fully committed to its vigorous protection.

What's next for the stock market? When will it pop? And how low will it go?

No one knows the future, but our model can show us some highly probable pathways.

Rising Interest Rates Will Kill the Bubble

Falling interest rates helped push the stock market bubble up, and, in reverse, rising interest rates will pull the stock market bubble down.

What will make interest rates rise?

The Federal Reserve does not want to raise rates. Doing so would only work to cool economic growth and spook the stock market at a time when the Fed has never been more committed to stimulating the economy and boosting the market during the Covid Crisis. Hence, it is unlikely that the Fed will move to raise interest rates a lot. Not now, not later, if they can avoid it.

But the Fed is not entirely in control of interest rates, especially after it has printed such massive amounts of money during the 2008–2009 Financial Crisis and much more during the 2020–2021 Covid Crisis.

As we described in Chapter 3, massive money printing is not risk-free. It will eventually lead to rising inflation. Not the mild and potentially short-term inflation we have today, but sustained, long-lasting high inflation.

At first, the Fed can and will do all it can to keep interest rates low, despite rising inflation. They can do this by printing more and more money. But if inflation is rising due to money printing (and it will), then you can see the problem. More money printing will just cause more inflation.

So, despite the Fed's desire to keep interest rates low to support the stock market, that goal will get harder and harder to achieve as inflation moves higher. At that point, the Fed can no longer hold interest rates down, and interest rates will have nowhere to go but up.

Until then, all is well. The Fed will keep printing and interest rates will stay low. But the longer the Fed is able to hold off rising interest rates, the worse the problem later.

Significant long-lasting inflation is still off in the future, but when it occurs, it is only a matter of time before interest rates rise as well. Any increase in interest rates, even modest increases, will punish bond holders and begin to scare stock investors. Initially, the stock market may not fall much, but the market's longest-running bull market will start to slow and eventually end. No crash, just no significant upward movement.

A non-bubble market could handle this period without much trouble, but for a bubble stock market lack of upward movement eventually becomes deadly. Bubbles must continue to rise, or they begin to fall.

Any significant market declines will likely be quickly met with even more massive government stimulus (money printing and borrowing). But eventually inflation will rise enough to make interest rates rise enough to pop the big Fake Money bubble we've been describing throughout this book – and that will include pushing the huge stock market bubble over the Financial Cliff.

Just How Low Will the Dow Go? Our Model Calculates the Amount

How low will the market ultimately fall?

We won't know until it actually occurs. But our model lets us look at what would happen to the stock market bubble using several assumptions of high interest rates, falling earnings and economic decline.

Animal Spirits Turn Deeply Negative

Although the big hits to the stock market will come from increases in interest rates and declining earnings and economic growth, the *first* big hit to the stock market will be from the decline in Animal Spirits – contributing about 21% to the overall fall, or roughly 5816 points.

How Much Will Negative Animal Spirits Pull the Dow Down?

Decline in Dow	Dow Level Remaining	Percentage of Decline Contributed
5816	22184	21%

On its own, the impact of positive Animal Spirits turning negative is not that large, compared to the total impact of all the market components turning negative and dragging the market down.

High Interest Rates Devastate the Market

High interest rates will destroy stock prices very quickly. Just as falling interest rates were the biggest driver pushing the stock bubble up, rising interest rates will have the same effect, only this time in reverse – and even more explosively.

In our model below (Table D.8), interest rates on corporate bonds shoot up from an average of 4% today to an average of 50% by 2030. This number is probably well below what will actually happen. At an interest rate rise to 50%, our model shows that the Dow will likely drop 70%.

Rising interest rates are, by far, the biggest factor in driving the market down, Remember, the key reason interest rates will rise is because inflation will rise due to money printing – and the Fed is going to do a lot of it.

Table D.8 How Much Will Rising Interest Rates Pull the Dow Down?

2021	2030	Dow Level Remaining	Percentage of Decline Contributed
4%	50%	2566	70%

Falling GDP Makes It Worse

GDP will decrease dramatically due to the near collapse of the capital goods sector and a huge drop in discretionary purchases. This dramatically affects the remaining Dow level, dropping it by over one half. But because it is already so low (as a result of the earlier interest rate rise), the portion of the total decline due to falling GDP will be relatively small.

How Much Will Falling GDP Pull the Dow Down?

Percentage Decline	Dow Level Remaining	Percentage of Decline Contributed
60%	1026	5%

Falling Profits Don't Help

The model also shows that the Dow will drop another 3% due to a two-thirds drop in corporate profits. Stocks are usually valued based on profits because a share of stock gives an investor the right to a share of the corporation's profit.

Profits normally increase at the same rate as GDP. In a boom, profit percentages increase, and in a recession they decrease. In this case, the profit percentage decreased from 6.4% to 2%, or about two-thirds, hurting the remaining stock market value.

In this case, that contributes 3% to the total decline of the Dow, which at this point is two-thirds of its remaining low value. The profit decline dramatically affects the remaining Dow level, but it is already so low as a result of the earlier interest rate rise that the portion of the total decline is relatively small.

How Much Will Falling Corporate Profits Pull the Dow Down?

2020	2030	Dow Level Remaining	Percentage of Decline Contributed
6.4%	2.0%	321	3%

All the Bubbles Pop

Remember, the stock market bubble is only part of the big Fake Money bubble we have been describing in this book. Stocks may be the first to plunge over the Financial Cliff, but they won't fall alone. The combined effects of high inflation and rising interest rates, will also pop the real estate bubble, decimate consumer spending, kill the bond market, and spike up unemployment as the economy dives into a deep recession.

And this time, the Fed's magic money printing won't save us. With previous massive money printing causing high inflation and high interest rates, the Fed will be forced to give it up. Massive borrowing will also be out. And for those who aren't prepared, a tremendous amount of wealth will disappear.

Fake Money in the past and present is setting us up for real danger in the future. For those who see it coming, there's still time to protect yourself.

Try Our Interactive Model Online

Want to see how different assumptions impact the bubble? Please visit the book's website, www.FakeMoneyRealDanger.com and click the navigation tab for "Interactive Bubble Insight Model." There you can play with the model's various inputs, such as the growth in the money supply, inflation rate, and other factors.

For example, the model can show you how money printing affects inflation, which impacts the nominal interest rate, which then changes the value of interest-rate-dependent assets, such as stocks, bonds, and real estate. By entering different data points, you will be able to see how each variable can change the timing and degree of the coming big bubble pop.

APPENDIX E

Questions and Answers Regarding Inflation (Chapter 3)

Since we approached the issue of when, or if, we will get inflation from a very different standpoint from almost all economists today on the left or right, we thought it would be useful to answer some of the frequently asked questions we get on inflation and our approach to it. It's an important issue, and our very different approach to inflation naturally draws a lot of questions. Some of those questions and answers are offered below:

QUESTION: What are the common measures of inflation used today? Which do you pay most attention to, and why?

ANSWER: Common measures include the Consumer Price Index, among others, but the numbers are not especially accurate because the government changes the basket of data to minimize inflation.

QUESTION: Are real increases in prices (e.g., due to increased demand) reflected in current measures of inflation?

ANSWER: Yes

QUESTION: Is it possible to back these out in order to see true inflation? When businesses raise prices, how do you distinguish between real price increases and inflation?

ANSWER: Good question. Real price increases tend to be temporary and decline as supply eventually increases to meet demand. True inflation doesn't disappear by increasing supply. Especially with stagflation, in which the economy is slow or slowing.

QUESTION: Do you have data that demonstrates that inflation historically lags money printing by 18–24 months but not since 2008?

ANSWER: The Federal Reserve has decades of studies in dozens of countries that demonstrate this inflation lag. As far as proof that it has not occurred since 2008, that's easy. There has been almost no inflation since 2008 despite massive money printing.

QUESTION: **Do you have data from other countries that demonstrates that the historical relationship between money printing and inflation still exists in countries other than the US?**

ANSWER: The Federal Reserve has lots of data on that. The studies we cited in the Fourth Edition of Aftershock on inflation from the Minneapolis Fed looked at multiple measures of money supply and multiple central banks.

QUESTION: **What do other economists think about modern monetary theory (MMT)?**

ANSWER: MMT is largely ignored by most mainstream liberal and conservative economists in academic discussions. However, MMT has become a popular issue in the business press, so we thought it was important to address it.

QUESTION: **How do non–modern monetary theory (MMT) economists explain the lack of inflation since 2008?**

ANSWER: Most economists think of inflation as a function of money printing. Hence, they are at a bit of a loss as to why we haven't gotten inflation. Some say that Paul Volcker killed inflation in the early 1980s and he did, but that doesn't explain what's happening today in the US with incredibly massive "free money" money printing. Also, other industrial nations are seeing the same phenomenon – lots of money printing and relatively little inflation in Japan, China, and Europe.

The lack of any solid explanation from mainstream economists, either liberal or conservative, is a large part of the reason there has been more focus on MMT, which tells us not to worry about trillion-dollar or multitrillion-dollar deficits. But, even MMT says we could get inflation at some point.

QUESTION: Do you have data that demonstrates that inflation is associated with low growth (stagflation) as opposed to rapid growth (overheating)?

ANSWER: The late 1970s through the early 1980s are a great example of low growth and high inflation. The 1950s are a great example of high growth and low inflation.

QUESTION: With stagflation, does inflation reduce economic growth, or does reduced growth cause inflation?

ANSWER: Stagflation is caused by a low-growth economy. When growth is low, governments tend to print more rather than raise taxes to cover increased social expenditures and reduced taxes. There is a feedback effect in that higher inflation will also cause slower growth due to higher interest rates and consumer fear.

QUESTION: What is excess reserve sterilization? Is this the Fed paying interest on excess reserves to encourage banks to hold them instead of lending them into economy?

ANSWER: Yes, the Fed pays interest on excess reserves to reward banks for limiting their lending. It was almost 2.5% in the middle of 2019 but was dropped to only 0.25% in March 2020, when the Covid crisis hit. Since then, it has gone even lower to 0.15% as of July 2021. If banks hold money in reserve rather than lending it out, they are "sterilizing" it by reducing the multiplier effect on the money supply from lending.

QUESTION: Historically, why have businesses raised prices about 18–24 months after money printing? What has been the

catalyst for price increases absent changes in demand, production costs, etc. (i.e., price increases due to inflation)?

ANSWER: Don't know. Good question. The normal lag factor research has not really focused on this issue. It simply looks at what happens when the Fed prints and how long it takes for inflation to show up.

QUESTION: Many pricing decisions are made by managers, not owners (e.g., in public or large private companies)? Does this impact your analysis at all?

ANSWER: Managers have the same motivations as owners. They want to keep making money. They want to support the bubble. Their bubble lifestyles depend on it, just as much as owners.

QUESTION: Do you have any data to suggest that business owners know we are in a bubble economy and that their actions will determine when the bubble will pop?

ANSWER: Business owners do not necessarily "know we are in a bubble." They just know that they feel anxious and want to keep the party going, rather than risk ending it. They also do not know that they will pop the bubble. They just know, if and when, the economy is doing poorly and they are getting hit, they try to offset the loss of sales by raising prices.

They are not analyzing the bubble or the bubble pop. They are trying to protect themselves, first by being in denial and later by trying to protect themselves. Just like stock investors. First denial, then fear. Both businesses and investors sense something needs protecting, even if they don't articulate that, even to themselves.

QUESTION: I definitely agree with your view that low inflation is required for continued massive stimulus (money printing and government borrowing) and that only significant inflation will force the end of stimulus and pop the bubble. I also agree that money printing alone is not sufficient to cause inflation; it must be accompanied by businesses deciding to raise prices.

However, I am struggling to accept your rationale regarding why businesses have not raised prices despite all the money printing. I freely admit that I do not have a better explanation, but I am skeptical that business owners understand we are in a stimulus-induced bubble economy and therefore have decided not to raise prices, even though all the factors that led businesses in the past to raise prices following money printing are presumably still in effect.

ANSWER: You are right, they don't understand. But they generally follow the same group behavior because of their shared group psychology, now and later. This is not mainstream economic thought, but we believe it is correct. Nothing else is as powerful an explanation.

Also, we see the same bubble-boosting psychological behavior in other areas of our bubble economy. For example:

Investors around the world are buying bonds with negative interest rates. NEGATIVE INTEREST RATES KEEP THE BUBBLES FROM BURSTING.

Banks in the US are holding massive excess reserves for the first time in more than 50 years. They never have held significant excess reserves in booms or busts. Banking 101 says that banks should lend out all they can to maximize profits. BUT HOLDING HUGE EXCESS RESERVES HELPS KEEP THE BUBBLES FROM BURSTING.

In a war, soldiers will take huge personal risks to help win the battle and the war. TAKING THOSE BIG PERSONAL RISKS HELPS KEEP THE COUNTRY FROM LOSING THE WAR.

Index